THE DIARY

A Complete Guide to Journal Writing

Curtis W. Casewit

ARGUS COMMUNICATIONS
A Division of DLM, Inc.
Allen, Texas 75002 U.S.A.

ACKNOWLEDGMENTS

Grateful acknowledgment is made to the following for material quoted in *The Diary: A Complete Guide to Journal-Writing:*

Unity Magazine and Frances Atkinson for quotations from "Diary of a Mountain Summer."

Katherine Sena for quotations from "Dolly's Legacy."

Doubleday & Company, Inc., for excerpts from *Anne Frank: The Diary of a Young Girl* by Anne Frank; copyright © 1952 by Otto H. Frank.

W. W. Norton & Company, Inc., for selections from *Recovering, A Journal* by May Sarton; copyright © 1980 by May Sarton.

Penguin Books Ltd. for excerpt from *Confessions* by Saint Augustine, translated by R. S. Pine-Coffin; copyright © R. S. Pine-Coffin, 1961.

Harper & Row, Publishers, Inc., for excerpt from *Pilgrim at Tinker Creek* by Annie Dillard; copyright © 1974 by Annie Dillard.

Cover Design and Cover Photograph by Joseph Essex

FIRST EDITION

Printed in the United States of America.

Argus Communications
A Division of DLM, Inc.
One DLM Park
Allen, Texas 75002 U.S.A.

International Standard Book Number: 0-89505-060-9
Library of Congress Number: 81-69698

Contents

Acknowledgments

A number of good and wise people have helped me with this book. Some of them did it indirectly, through their philosophies.

I want to thank Dr. George Bach, a psychiatrist who recommends honesty, honesty before all, between human beings. I'm grateful to Dr. Rollo May; I've read his works and corresponded with him. His overall depth is admirable. I need to thank John McPhee of the *New Yorker* for his encouraging letters. Dr. Sidney Werkman, a long-time friend, assisted me generously with this manuscript.

My gratitude also goes to Dr. John Young, psychiatrist and poet; to psychotherapist Trudy Helmlinger; to author John Malo; to Stephen Daoud Casewit, adventurer and diarist; to John M. Allen, editor and executive at the *Reader's Digest,* and to Frances Atkinson, a writer who underestimates her literary abilities. Katherina Sena, author of "Mom: Dolly's Legacy," shared the death of her mother with me. Jerry Hunter did some additional research for this book. It is dedicated to Helen E.

Denver, Colorado *C.C.*

1

The Diary and You

Introduction

The other day, while doing research for this book, I happened to rummage through some cellar shelves. And there in the dusty half-darkness, I found a manila envelope stuffed with tiny notebooks. A half dozen of them. My first diaries—

I opened one. "May 12," I read. "Played soccer with Max today." Max and I were eight years old then. The notebook covers were bent with age, the paper yellowed. My doings at ages ten and twelve were recorded on lined pages. Almost daily entries. Brief ones. About school, a teacher, classmates. About a trip with my father. About a lonely Christmas.

Anyone can keep a journal of sorts. Small children do it all the time. So do adolescents of both genders, and, of course, the adults. It doesn't take writing ability. Spelling and grammar? Many diarists create their own. It merely requires willingness to sit down and to make some occasional entries. These can be short.

Thus: "It must be spring. Last week, the boys were still racing across the ice surface of our little neighborhood lake. Today I saw them tossing rocks into the waters. And the pussy willows were beginning to show their little white faces . . . ."

I've always kept diaries, consigning some of my war experiences to paper as well. And so, on November 10, 1940, while only nineteen but already a soldier, I wrote: "I'm opening my diary once more. A brief self-interview. What would I like to do just now? Ah, to travel! To get out of this military zone! To eat well just once, to hear good music—"

Your sallies into the outdoors, your travels, and professional travails are all grist for the diary mill. I set down my early days as a bachelor, followed by an account of my marriage. Later, I wrote about the baby's first smiles and the growth of our other children.

Novelist Ivan Doig once stated that a diary allows us to "touch life as it flows." This is so true.

Although our libraries contain the journals of poets, philosophers, diplomats, religious leaders, authors, explorers—and many others—a diary is a personal thing and normally not for publication. Consider Anne Frank, the Dutch girl who wrote such a moving account of her (and her family's) years of hiding during World War II. She never intended her diary to become a book, let alone a best seller. One of her entries: "I hope I shall be able to confide in you completely, as I have never been able to do in anyone before, and I hope that you will be a great support and comfort to me."

In short, you commit your own private observations, meditations, ruminations to paper. Every entered word is up to you. If you want to, you can put down trivia. You can also, as many of us must do at some time in our lives, explore a personal tragedy. Whatever you write, you can confide it to your journal. "It was my only steadfast friend," wrote the late Anaïs Nin. And one Nobel Prize-winning author called his journal "a true confidant, to whom I can tell every secret—"

The Diary Versus the Journal: A Definition

Webster's definition of the journal: "A daily record of personal activities, reflections of feelings." And Webster on the diary: "From *dies* (day). A record of events, transactions, or observations, kept daily or at frequent intervals." In these pages, *journal* and *diary* will be used interchangeably. (Both are also "a book of dated entries.") May Sarton, that superb novelist, poet, and diarist, collects her creative ideas in a "journal." Yet if you look at the dates, not every day is represented. Several weeks may go by before she returns to writing. Nobel Prize-winning André Gide, a superb diarist, sometimes went for weeks without making an entry. Yet he too spoke of his "journals" and not of his diaries. More definitions? One teacher says the two words mean the same thing. But they're "receptacles for writing down tomorrow's memories." Another diarist simply calls his journal a "savings account for recollections." So be it.

The Many Worlds of the Journal

The recollections can merely describe what you did on a certain day. Some people have written down recipes. A supervisor of a weight-reducing plan recommends that you record your daily weight and what you ate.

Or consider these other myriad possibilities for your journal:

- The comings and goings of friends.
- A description of things you've just bought. (Emerson would even report in his journal how much he paid for each item.)
- A brief opinion about a book you've just read.
- Movies (or plays) you've recently seen and your reactions to them.
- A rash letter to someone, the kind of letter you really don't want to send.
- An idea about improving the condition of a family member, a citizen in your community, or even the country.
- An unusual encounter with another person.
- Details on the seeds you recently planted or on the crop you harvested or on the plants or flowers you just bought. (Thoreau was very good at such details.)
- Data on birds you've watched or animal tracks in the snow or views of a changing landscape.
- Some calculations about money coming in and going out. Perhaps even tentative figures for a personal budget.
- A birthday and how you spent it and felt about it.
- Errands you've run that day and their outcome.
- Sketches. Photographs. Collages.
- Shopping lists.
- An important thought. "Without hope, it is impossible to find the unhoped for," writes Heraclitus. Dr. Viktor Frankl: "The salvation of man is only through love and in love—"

- A personal credo.
- Figures that interest you. Emerson's journals contain dollar figures for the cost of a local monument, the income of a local aristocrat, and the fee received by a concert pianist of the times.

The list could still go on. For instance: How about notes on football, baseball, basketball, tennis, skiing, swimming, or running? (Complete with scores that may be intriguing ten years from now.) Or for the animal lover, a few occasional words about the antics of your house cat(s) or dog(s)? And wouldn't some New Year's resolutions fit into the last days of December? (These resolutions could be reviewed twelve months later!) Also, how about recording (or creating) some prayers?

An observation might fit in very well, too. "I love St. Peter's Church," Emerson wrote on April 7, 1883, in Rome. "It is an ornament of the earth. It should be called the sublime of the beautiful."

Even some up-to-date material on the present is one possibility. When working on this book about diaries, for instance, I made the following (then current) entry:

> The rented condo really proves ideal for my purposes. No phone. No mail. No newspapers with horror stories. Not even a TV set, which further guarantees peace. No dogs barking. No people dropping in. What more could a writer ask for? And all around, long, tree-lined paths for long walks. In short, a blissful situation. Result? Fifty more pages on the new book . . . .

The present becomes even more interesting in faraway places. An American trekked through the Himalayas, for instance. He had had almost no writing experience until then. But he kept a diary. He later shared it with me, and I couldn't help marveling at his natural writing talent. How well he described his impressions! What remarkable accuracy! A brief sample:

> Pitched camp between Ghandrung and Chomrong early. Mighty mountains loom about, a river rushes along, a heavy drum and mournful horn still echo through the hills chasing a funeral procession of some sort. My feet are blistered and sore but my muscles are hard. Marching up steep steps and down treacherous slopes, over mountains, through parched valleys of blazing white stone, above pounding streams, through jungles and across rice paddies, over precarious bridges, past grazing buffalo . . . .

Some writers devote much space to their thoughts about other people. And, of course, human beings make fascinating subjects. An employee may be irked at his/her superior; the diary becomes a fine outlet for analyzing the boss, for looking at this person from all angles. Or is your job too much? Did you have a particularly difficult day? If so, it will make you feel better to comment on it. People? A man of my acquaintance filled most of his diary pages with observations—and not always loving ones—about his long-time spouse. And she did the same thing! A form of communication. (Alas, the couple failed to share the diaries with each other.)

Even the journals of the most profound, observant individuals often examine some of the more pleasant (or less serious) aspects of life.

Poet and novelist May Sarton, for instance, sometimes begins with the weather. An example:

> Home to pouring rain and a rich green world here. Tulips are over, cherries almost, but the lilacs are in

full bloom and scent the air in the rain. I have been on a real holiday, far away, for two weeks, on a barge on the Thames, in London.

Rich Corazza, an Alaskan homesteader-trapper, used his journal to catalogue how many weasels (he spelled it "weazels") he shot that particular morning, or how many rabbits wound up in his snares. He wrote about finding lynx tracks in the snow, about (unsuccessfully) hunting moose and going after grouse with a pistol at 35 degrees below zero. We must thank John McPhee, of the *New Yorker*, for the discovery of the homesteader's notes. An illustration:

Saturday, December 13

The weather has been -50 or lower (-60 was the lowest) for 12 days but this morning the wind started blowing and the weather warmed up some 40° to -8. I ran the dogs down across the river to get a load of fish yesterday.

Although he lived alone in the remote Yukon mountain cabin, the man wrote only about the external events in his life. He gave us a good picture of frozen Yukon rivers, of the daily temperatures, and the cutting/storing of wood for survival. However briefly, he recorded the outer dimension of his life.

Other diarists prefer to describe the shapes and colors of what they see, again with only a minimum of internalizing. For instance:

Winter Park, Colorado *September 24*

A day to remember. Never did the leafy forest shine brighter and the mountain crests sharper. Nature seemed to indulge in one last autumn festival—red bushes (blood red), golden aspen, pink aspen, white-green sage—all under the bluest sky.

Good to be alive.

An Inward Journey

A diary may also be used to reveal a person's inner life. Some of our joys are too much to bear. Our triumphs, our sudden spiritual insights, along with the normal stresses and anxieties, all call out for pen and paper. The diary then becomes the letter to yourself.

It is true that many people reach for their journals mostly when life's tide suddenly buffets them. Ilse, a middle-aged woman—a nonwriter—learned one sad day that her thirty-year-old son had died in an automobile accident. The pain made her reach for a somewhat neglected diary. "I poured out my feelings," she says. "I'm grateful that I had the chance. Everyone ought to do it." Everyone could benefit from diary-writing.

Ilse had no literary ambitions; she wrote just as she spoke. Style? No matter. A neat handwriting? Unimportant; only she had to decipher it later on.

Journal-writing proves its true worth when we face inner turmoil. A forty-year-old single man who had unsuccessfully sought a deep love relationship reveals his continuing quest. "But the hollow heart remains," he writes. "One hopes in vain for a deeper sharing. A give and take, validation. But in the end, those modern relationships are only surface. I refuse to adapt. Surely, we cannot give in and lower our values to a tenth of a loaf? Surely, we who *are* deep, who are made for the more intimate bond, surely we must continue our quest for it?"

"A friend! A friend!" the main character cries out in Romain Rolland's *Jean-Christophe*. "A friend!" And Rolland added wisely, "How many friends do we have in a lifetime? Three? Two? One?"

We must search for them.

The diary furnishes this single man with the intimacy he needs and the opportunity to come close to his *self.* He has read about the frequent lack of deeper relations between men and women. And he finds great satisfaction in quoting Dr. Rollo May and Dr. George Bach, two psychiatrists who address themselves to these problems. A recent diary entry: "Dr. May said somewhere that the easier sex is come by, the more difficult is the true deep communion, while Dr. Bach stresses that intimacy is more important than ever, now that we're 'faceless numbers on a list. . . .' He also explains, with great lucidity, just *why* we need closeness, why deep love, why true intimacy has become so important. It provides, he says, 'The feelings of worth and identity that preserve sanity and meaning. . . .' And he poignantly concludes, 'One hungers for a pair of eyes to give us true recognition and acceptance, for one heart that understands and can be understood—'"

"Amen."

Like no other tool, the diary helps to explore our feelings, our private struggles, as well as our peak experiences. We permit ourselves that much-needed pause to meditate. Ah, how rewarding to be alone for a reflective moment! And how well this solitude can be used for that journey inward, or even backward!

Return to the Past

To be sure, diary pages can be reread at some later time. One author already knows this when he, as he puts it, sets down "shamelessly and at length certain lamentations in the hope of learning something from them . . . ." Ilse, the woman who lost her son, was later grateful that she shared the sorrow with her journal. "If I hadn't put down my feelings, I would never have known how much I loved him," she says. "You forget so much! But the diary is a mirror." And listen to the late Anaïs Nin, no doubt one of the world's most famous and prolific diarists. At the age of thirty, she wrote: "Dear Diary: You've kept me alive as a human being." In all, she kept a journal for fifty years. And for many decades, she gave lectures to large audiences about the contents of her long-ago journals.

The memory-bank aspects affect all ages and nationalities. A busy American magazine executive expresses his regret that he himself never got around to keeping a journal. But he adds: "My daughter of eleven keeps a diary every night—and I envy her greatly, for she will always have the opportunity of looking back and remembering and recapturing moments that have already slipped into my subconscious."

In the best sense, you can relive—rediscover!—some important events in your past.

Romain Rolland, the French author, once observed that "when the present seems unendurable, it is time to look backward." This can be done through the pages of your journal. Some long-gone days may still gleam there as if you had just experienced them. Ah, precious moments of a year ago! Such reliving through rereading can bring double happiness.

An illustration? Kathy Sena, a young New England woman, had never attempted any writing at all except for some letters. But one day, in the grip of emotion, she decided to recapture her special feelings in a diary.

Among her first entries:

Tuesday

I do believe God planned this beautiful day for me—and—it was perfection.

Thank you. Thank you. Thank you, Jesus . . . .

I'm so full of Love for Life now and I must follow my dream. People are beautiful, life is beautiful, and the feelings that I have in me now are overwhelming and I have to share life and enjoy it to the fullest.

I love so strongly and if I get hurt by it—it's better to love and to be hurt than to never have felt love and life. I have so much love to give from the smallest creature to the smallest flower that the highest obstacle is out of my reach now. I will bask in God's favor and enjoy his grace because he *is* and he alone will guide me!

2

How to Start Your Diary

Physical Format

The choice is entirely up to you. A five-and-ten cent store sells notebooks of various sizes. Small ones fit into the pockets of a traveler. A steno pad is fine; the lines prove useful in guiding those who don't write often. A novice will also feel comfortable with a large calendar, the kind that offers one full page per day. Blank books that are normally used for school use, with or without spirals, in softcover or hardcover, also lend themselves to journal-writing. (An accountant of my acquaintance even uses a ledger.)

Book stores often sell more elaborate items. Diaries that lock. Gingham-bound diaries. Even clothbound ones from China, which have pagodas and exotic trees on the covers. (All that at only eight dollars.) Most bookshops also carry an increasingly popular hardcover item that makes a good journal. It's *The Nothing Book*. Cooked up by a mass-market publisher, the book has about two hundred blank pages with or without lines, as you wish. *The Nothing Book* is subtitled *Want to Make Anything of It?* and costs just a few dollars; the same house also publishes *The Anything Book*.

Artists' diaries are available in art-supply shops. For the very rich, there is the Gucci refillable desk-size journal at a scandalous $150. People who want personal diaries but who don't like to write—like a wealthy lady I know—can resort to a tape recorder. This particular lady talks into it and her secretary later types it all up.

This leads to one more choice: you can write in your journal in longhand or, as I often do, type on separate sheets and then paste these into the journal. No matter. It's *your* diary, so who can tell you what to do?

The Beginner's Guide to Getting Started

Starting a diary, and writing in it "is as easy as breathing," the late Anaïs Nin told us many years ago. And diarist May Sarton once confessed that "it's almost too easy."

This is true, of course, for nearly any person who knows the alphabet. If one can keep a message, a shopping list, or a letter, one can also keep a diary. The time investment is minimal; an entry need take only minutes. (You're writing for yourself and not for a Nobel Prize in literature.)

Some privacy seems more important. Your child (or children) should be in another room, your spouse or friend absent for the moment. Find a calm time in your room, or look for peace and quiet outdoors under the sun or in the shade of a tree. "Solitude is the richness of the self," goes one saying. (Loneliness is something else again.)

I don't believe that it takes inspiration to inscribe a few lines in your journal. You merely sit down; the first words will come, like the morning's dew. Of course, if you just experienced a great joy—or a tragedy—there may be veritable word rivers.

Seasoned diarists agree that it is always best to set down your thoughts at once. Don't wait for days until you have digested an experience. Describe it when it is fresh. Impressions? Philosophical reflections? Anxieties or worries? Suspicions? Pin them all down in your journal as soon as you can. Waiting means forgetting; a delay may pale whatever you felt.

According to one of his biographers, Emerson's "method was to write down in the heat of vision the truth as it seemed to him at the moment . . . ." Emerson lived from 1803 to 1882. His method is still valid for the twentieth century.

We saw in the previous chapter that the diarist can select both material and format. The diary can be made up of trivia or of bare facts. The trick is not to hesitate. Just sit down and write rapidly. Don't worry about the correctness of words at this stage. Simply get it down on paper.

A twenty-one-year-old traveler had a few thoughts about his stay in Alaska:

> Felt overcome by glee and amusement that I was once again boarding a plane, once again seeking new adventures. Three months ago I sat on these same airport lounge chairs wondering what sort of hand fate would deal me. Here I am a quarter-year later. I replenished my dwindling funds with $600. I amassed a wealth of knowledge on specific Alaskan people.
>
> I gathered a clearer impression of the fishing industry. I was exposed to many new influences. Though I will

never be twenty again, I shall not regret that I spent part of the precious period in Kodiak.

A journal can wander. Detours *are* permissible. Nijinsky, the dancer, would cover a dozen locales, thoughts, impressions, and points in a single page. Other diarists prefer to conjure up the colors, smells, and sounds of the moment or of an hour ago and then report in depth.

Certainly, the writer can ask questions. What did you feel? What was your gut reaction? Were there physical reactions to an event? Which words were spoken in a human encounter? Or how about the texture of a landscape? And the mood of it? How would a painter depict it? And so on.

Journals are often born in stressful situations. A well-known politician is charged with tax fraud by the U.S. government and sentenced to fifty days in jail. A diary—his first!—emerges with ease. His emotions are strong enough—his impressions powerful enough—for almost daily writing.

A young woman showed me a diary about her mother's grave illness. The woman had never written a journal before. But the diary about the beloved parent almost wrote itself. Emotion provided the wings. No one has to take a writing course to describe illness and death.

Here is an excerpt from Kathy Sena's journal:

Thursday, August 23

I headed toward Boston, not knowing for one minute it would be my last trip to the hospital to be with Mom. As I walked into the hospital I met one of my mother's doctors. When we got off the elevator he squeezed my shoulder. "Go to your mother," he said. "She had a bad night. She needs you." My heart was

> pounding as I walked into the room. The nurse's face told the story. Then the nightmare of my life was here, the end of my mother's life. Mom was in a partial coma. But she was trying to say something. "It's all right," I whispered, and held her hand. My mother quieted and seemed to go into a deep sleep.
>
> Later, one of the nurses told me that my mother may be passing. I reached for Mom's hand again. I felt it change from warm to cold.
>
> Then she was gone. But she will never be really gone. . . . Her legacy to me is the legacy of love.

How Often Should You Write?

Kathy Sena wrote these words in the throes of emotion; she also wrote almost daily about the illness that led to her mother's final moments. Later, after Kathy recovered, she began to use her diary to report on her marriage, to ponder about her children. Much went on, so she wrote every day. Later, just once a week.

How about your own preferences? E. J. Kahn, the *New Yorker* magazine journalist, was known to make writing in his journal a daily ritual. There is no compelling reason why you should have to; on the other hand, the daily dedication has advantages for newcomers. Writing teachers keep telling prospective authors that they should write something—anything!—*every day,* so as to get used to the written word. In the same sense, daily diary-writing makes you more familiar with the process. You're bound to become more articulate. You'll also get more deeply into the diary habit than if you made entries only once a year.

How much should you write when you do? The quantity is up to you; even one paragraph will do.

Here is Emerson:

> *December 21, 1828*
>
> I have now been four days engaged to Ellen Louisa Tucker. Will my Father in Heaven regard us with kindness, and as he hath, as we trust, made us for each other, will he be pleased to strengthen & purify & prosper & eternize our affection!

Emerson waited until January 17—more than three weeks!—to record his next thoughts, this time about "the purity and angelic religion" of his fiancée.

Frequency may be less important than writing when you have deep feelings about something or when the new thought presses hard against your brain walls and you must get it on paper. At some point, you will miss writing—if you're besieged by obligations or work, for instance—and those inner prods will eventually lead you back to your journal.

André Gide didn't write for weeks when he was ill or saddened by the wartime occupation of France or engaged in a demanding translation of Shakespeare. But eventually he always returned to his journal, if only with twenty or thirty entries a year. May Sarton's fine diaries come with long silences; these are mostly her travel periods. (Or she gives university lectures and has no strength left.) Other diarists—like me, for instance—go to their journals only when they have intense feelings, being either upset about something or greatly pleased by an experience or turn of events.

Bear in mind that journal-writing, like many other things in life, takes a certain discipline; you're allowed your days off (or even a week). But then you must go back to your pages. There are far too many amateur novelists who want to write a novel but never do, or who get as far as chapter one and then abandon the project. Ditto for diarists. You must get on with it and do it. Says one wit: "If you wait for inspiration, you're not a writer but a waiter." On the other hand, there is nothing wrong with jotting down a single line as I did on November 30, 1941, in this wartime confession: "I don't have the patience to write today. Maybe tomorrow." Your options are appealing indeed. Length and frequency can vary and you don't even have to stick to a strict chronology. Napoleon Bonaparte's valet explained this in an 1811 journal:

> I have no intention, in this journal, of conforming to a very exact order of dates; and whenever there recurs to my memory a fact or an anecdote that seems to me deserving of mention, I shall jot it down, at whatever point of my narrative I may have then reached, fearing lest, should I defer it to its proper epoch, it might be forgotten.

A writer may occasionally put down older memories in what are known as flashbacks; others prefer to name the days instead of chronological dates (Monday, Tuesday, etc.).

How about the best time to start? Some individuals swear by January 1, but that important day doesn't necessarily guarantee continued success. An acquaintance puts it this way: "Dear Curtis: As a matter of fact, I don't keep a diary on a regular basis. I start one in January and, I fear, lose interest."

In short, there are no rules. And even if there were, the amateur diarist need not stick to them. For others, especially those who write for a living, a journal can become an addiction—a place where they're free to be themselves.

Length of Entries

A while back, we noticed how Emerson was able to express, in a mere five lines, his great affection for his future wife. Those five lines are still vivid today, some 150 years later. Some diarists may toss off thoughts even in just one or two lines.

In 1930, a middle-aged novelist registered this familiar complaint in his journal: "I ought to give up smoking. As I write these words, I light another cigarette—"

A mature eighteen-year-old American in Paris meanwhile grapples with the same problem. But he devotes more journal space to it and reaches a different conclusion:

> *Samedi à Paris*
>
> My tug of war with tobacco has ended. In a sudden fit of inspiration, I seized my pipe and flung it from the balcony of my room into an empty park below. The tobacco itself I showered onto the sidewalk. It is quite early (4:30 A.M.). The Paris sky is a dark-pastel gray. My tongue still feels seared by the pipe I smoked last night in the Le Dôme cafe. My lungs feel poached. It is high time I left this self-destructive habit to others.
>
> I feel it is O.K. to savor an occasional cigar *after* a fine dinner or to taste a cigarette among friends now and then—but to own a tiny smoke factory of my own and to make prodigious use of it must be taboo. That is self-pollution.
>
> My lungs were not made for smoking. I can no longer ignore my body's warnings. I do not want to be a coughing, hacking old man. I must defeat my most debilitating weakness.

The length of each entry is up to the writer. Anaïs Nin could carry on for many pages that added up more to a long memoir than to a journal. It took Ms. Nin six volumes and some 150,000 pages to finish her chronological autobiography. A British naval official, Samuel Pepys, who lived from 1633 to 1703, found the time to produce a diary of 1,300,000 words, often in long, awkward segments. It was his hobby, and no one could dissuade him; in the end, his diaries still prove useful to present-day historians. Pepys needed wordage. But he also gave us rich descriptions—of London's Great Fire, for instance.

Brevity can be effective, too.

An aging woman summons the honesty to write:

> *February 10, 1980*
>
> I just realized a very sad thing. "The First Time," a song by Roberta Flack, is playing. It used to be that when I heard this song, cold chills would go through me and a special person would appear in my mind. Now there is nothing, just emptiness.

And Kathy Sena, some weeks after her mother's passing:

> The Lord gives and the Lord takes away and I must accept that he has taken Ma and she now resides with him, her Father and mine, and someday I shall also be with him and the great reunion of seeing Mom's beautiful smile once again. As I am also guided by his hand.

The right number of words seems less important than whether the sentences later bring back the scene of your sensations. Here are some brief observations from my own diaries. One took six lines; the next entry only two lines. Both still remind me of the contentment I felt in those long-ago October days:

> *October 2*
>
> A hike:
> Magnificent Indian Summer day!

We hike the Mesa Trail from Eldorado Springs. The colors—the golds and reds and oranges—are sending me into aesthetic highs. Up and down and through forests, meadows—four miles. And how good the cold tea tastes afterward!

October 4

Even today, two days later, the colors are still under my eyelids. Ah, rewarding, haunting nature!

Style and the Diarist

You're writing for yourself and not for publication. Style is therefore of no importance. You're not being graded by a professor.

In fact, a journal doesn't have to be well-written. Don't worry much about syntax or grammar, or even about correct spelling. The homesteader's diary found by John McPhee in Alaska packed greater interest than many an academician's journal. The hermit didn't spell well, yet he told all we needed to know about the Yukon hardships. His lesson of survival comes through loud and clear.

Long before him, the pioneers headed West kept dated notes that can still have an impact today. Spelling? Never mind. "We came near being drounded," wrote a young Mormon girl en route to Utah in 1856. "*Drounded?*" And why not? We know she meant *drowned.* And Ira Progoff, who knows more about journals than most other people in our century, points out at his Intensive Journal Workshops that "literacy is a minor factor." In fact, this psychologist has conducted very productive workshops in ghetto areas for people with little writing experience. "Their inner lives are rich," says Progoff. "And therefore their journal experiences are both creative and profound."

Accurate spelling becomes important only if you write for publication; in that case, editors frown upon too many errors. (A good dictionary will prove helpful.) Luckily, diaries are not generally rewritten, and they shouldn't be. If you wait for the right word, or later go back for a lot of editing, your diary will no longer be spontaneous, no longer natural. By the same token, professional magazine writers or book authors rewrite and revise a great deal; they often aim at perfection.

Some new diarists actually write just as they speak. There is nothing wrong with this. The crucial thing is to get your thoughts on paper. No matter if the sentences turn out to be long or short. Or if your paragraphs are long or short. Your journal entries should be unself-conscious. In *Recovering: A Journal,* May Sarton makes this point, too:

> I have worked toward a transparent style, as simple and plain as possible, a tool with which to communicate complex relationships. When I began to write I was praised for a "poetic style," but it is just that I have tried to get rid of as too self-conscious. I have come to believe that too elaborate a style gets in the way, dazzles but makes a wall between writer and reader.

Natural writing can also be achieved by means of casting your journal entries as letters. Anne Frank, the Dutch girl who'd never kept a diary before, did just that; she called her diary Kitty and Anne wrote to her "Dear Kitty" almost every day. More suggestions? You can also use the third person if you wish.

Julius Caesar chose that form to describe his Gallic Wars. Here is an illustration of Caesar's third-person *Commentaries:*

> Caesar, having moved forward from Auximum, traversed the whole country of Picenum. All the governors in these countries most cheerfully received him, and aided his army with every necessity. Embassadors came to him even from Cingulum, a town that Labieanus had laid out and built at his own expense, and offered most earnestly to comply with his orders. He demanded soldiers; they sent them. In the meantime, the twelfth legion came to join Caesar; with these two he marched to Asculum, the chief town of Picenum.

Honesty

Only professional authors write for the public. Because you don't write for others, you can say anything you like. You can be totally frank with yourself on how you perceive other people and what you really think about yourself. For once, you can shed that official mask that most Americans wear for their daily lives. You can't blame us; it is the Anglo-Saxon heritage that forbids us to reveal our innermost feelings. We must keep the stiff upper lip, as the British call it, even at a point when our lives teeter or fall apart. "And how are *you* today?" a co-worker or an acquaintance asks. "Oh, fine, just fine!" you say, despite the severe arthritic pains or the money worries or personal problems.

Americans are expected to be positive at all costs. "Letting it all hang out" is for the weak or the neurotic or for small children. An example? A long-time friend, upon my asking how his little firm was doing, told me repeatedly that "business is terrific." But by chance I found out that he was close to bankruptcy and that he had lost, in fact, most of his business. Masks!

The diary is a different cup of tea altogether. You can be candid, for there are no censors of private journals.

This is especially true when it comes to feelings—the sort you don't want to share with another person. Author George Sand demonstrated this some 150 years ago. This sensitive, nineteenth-century woman reveals what it's like to love someone and not be loved in return. Her entry of November 25, 1834, has that honesty that gives true meaning to journal-writing:

> Sometimes I am tempted to go to his house and pull on his doorbell until the cord breaks. Sometimes I imagine myself lying down outside his door waiting for him to come out. I would like to fall at his feet—no, not at his feet—that would be madness—but I would like to throw myself into his arms and cry out, "Why do you deny your love for me?"

You can speak not only about unrequited love but also about your fears, anguish, loneliness, incompleteness, the hungers for a human touch. Indeed, the best journals are those that focus on an individual's true inner world. You might call the entries a safety valve. The diary gives us a chance to let off steam, to let go of angers we can't show in public. Franz Kafka thus wrote frankly about his disenchantment with his father. André Gide used his diary to talk back to his many critics; Gide spoke of "purging himself" through his journals. May Sarton is unafraid to express self-doubt about her work; she tells her journal about a faltering love affair. Thanks to such openness, the diary became (in her words) a "way of sorting myself out—and climbing out of a depression."

Psychiatrists consider such openness a very healthy thing; moreover, they say that a release of your feelings is beneficial. Freud initially called psychoanalysis a "talking cure"; this also applies to your "talking it all out" in writing. (More of this in chapter 4, "The Diary: What Psychiatrists and Psychologists Say.")

As always, the format for your honest self-analysis is up to you. It could be a letter to someone or to yourself. It could be in the form of a poem, written as best you can. (It doesn't have to rhyme; few modern poems do.)

You can also use your private journal for a pro-and-con list. If you really put all your thoughts on the line, such a list helps you make an important decision. The following is an illustration from the diary of a thirty-year-old man who tried to decide whether he should stay married. He honestly weighs the pros and cons of divorce:

Why we should stay together

For children's sake.
Divorce would be financially difficult.
My deep roots in house (17 years).
Affection and admiration for my wife.
Her basic need to be married.
Great inconvenience of moving.
So far no replacement for her.
Fear of loneliness.
I'm being *well* taken care of.
Prospect of old age.
Social disapproval; divorce stigma.
Pending divorce trauma.

Why we should separate

Too many scars on her side.
Too much bitterness on her side.
Grown apart.
Physical indifferences on both sides.

Deep need for love on my part (unfulfilled for years).
My craving for adventure.
Search for youth.
Need for freedom.
Her unforgiveness.
Chronic (undeserved) distrust.

These considerations were very personal ones, applying only to this individual. But their candor is obvious. And such lists fit perfectly into a journal. Reason? The writer gains perspective and later learns much from what he or she wrote and did.

Some new diarists may be a little afraid to commit such private thoughts to paper. What if a spouse, a companion, a family member should find the diary and then read all these confidential thoughts?

These questions make sense, of course. A diary is a private matter and for your eyes alone. If a person lives with someone else, such privacy may not be simple to come by. But it is essential for the diarist. Young or old, you need to find an appropriate hiding place for your journal. It can be locked into a fireproof cashbox. Some people own small safes. Every apartment or house has all kinds of possible stashing places. It just takes a little imagination to know the right drawer, shelf, box, lockable suitcase, typewriter case. Seek and ye shall find!

On occasion, the most private thoughts *can* fall into the hands of another person. A colleague of mine, a man, had a hard time expressing his great love for his wife. He was too inhibited, too enclosed to talk about it. But he was eventually able to confide this love to his diary.

One day, by chance, his wife found it. She was very pleased.

3

The Diary as a Chronicle

A Diversity of Diarists

Through the ages, a massive number of journals have been written by all kinds of persons in many languages. The editor of one modern anthology read some 1200 diaries for possible inclusion in a book. And when you check your library, you become aware of the diversity of people who have kept journals. It seems that not only the butcher, the baker, and the candlestick maker have filled these volumes. But your librarian can also point to the day-by-day memoirs of Queen Victoria, Davy Crockett, Countess Tolstoy, Lord Byron, the dancer Nijinsky, feminist George Sand, Charles Robert Darwin, Jean Paul Sartre, and Mark Twain, to name just a few people.

As we shall see, diaries are the logical outlet for writers, for painters, and for other artists. We learn much about Leonardo da Vinci through his diaries. Gauguin, the great Impressionist, chronicled his own life, and the unhappy van Gogh expressed himself via letters to his brother Theo—letters that resembled sections of a diary.

In more recent times, perhaps ten years ago, we learned about the artistry of the so-called wild Sioux Indians through the 1852 journals of a Swiss artist named Rudolph Friedrich Kurz. The Swiss visitor kept a detailed account about an Indian visiting him in Yellowstone country. "I was sketching that afternoon," Kurz wrote. "To my surprise, the Sioux brought along two interesting drawings of his own. While I worked he glanced over my shoulder and nodded rather sympathetically. It turned out, however, that he was not at all satisfied with my drawings. He explained to me that he could do better." Many years later, the German artist Käthe Kollwitz (1867-1945) kept voluminous chronological notes that give us an insight into why and how she created the posters for which she became famous. ("There must be understanding between the artist and the people," she wrote.) Much of her work was fueled by the wars she hated and by her social conscience; she became known for her drawings of the hungry and the poor. Social scientists have often catalogued their thoughts in their journals. So have scientists and explorers, of course.

Scientists and Explorers

The diary often becomes essential for the geologist, the physicist, the chemist, the physician, the inventor. How else would we know the route taken by Madame Curie in her study of radioactivity? How else could we have learned about the step-by-step inventions of an Edison or a Ford? And many of the early advances in medicine, the first great exploits in surgery, came to us via journals.

To be sure, we'd have no record of exploration if it were not for the logbooks of long-ago voyagers such as Christopher Columbus; this discoverer of America had kept shipboard records in 1492. (Interestingly, Columbus insisted on keeping two separate logs—an optimistic one for the crew and a more honest one, with some of his own trepidations, for himself.)

Thanks to journals, we learned about Hernando Cortes's exploits in Mexico during the sixteenth century. And Ferdinand Magellan (1480-1521) comes to us through some interesting journals kept by an Italian who sailed the oceans with him. Centuries later, the 1869 diaries of Major John Wesley Powell and of his men gave us a first look at the wild Colorado River and the bottom of the Grand Canyon. Powell, a professor of natural history, was thirty-five years old when he set out on behalf of the U.S. government to map these unknown regions and to make geographical studies. Major Powell and his fellow explorers kept a careful chronicle of their complicated and hazardous voyage, much of it by boat. The pioneer party recorded their harrowing adventure:

> *June 8*
>
> At the foot of one of these runs, early in the afternoon I found a place where it would be necessary to make a portage, and signaling the boats to come down, I walked along the bank to examine the ground for the portage. But five minutes after I heard a shout, and looking around, I saw one of the boats coming over the falls. Capt. Howland had not seen any signal in time, and the swift current carried him to the brink. His going over was inevitable.

> The first fall was not great, only two or three feet, and we had often run such, but below it continued to tumble down twenty to thirty feet more, in a channel filled with rocks that broke the waves into whirlpools and beat them into foam. I turned just to see the boat strike a rock and throw the men and cargo out. Still they clung to her sides and clambered in again and saved part of the oars, but she was full of water, and they could not manage her. Still down the river they went, two or three hundred yards to another rocky rapid just as bad, and the boat struck again amidships, and was dashed to pieces. The men were thrown into the river and carried beyond my sight.

According to the diary, the men were saved, but all their instruments, extra clothes, and rations were lost.

Another time, the major describes a scary climb that gets him and a companion stuck on a precarious rock.

> I find I can get up no farther, and cannot step back, for I dare not let go with my hand, and cannot reach foothold below without. I call to Bradley for help. He finds a way by which he can get to the top of the rock over my head, but cannot reach me. Then he looks around for some stick or limb of a tree, but finds none. Then he suggests that he had better help me with the barometer case; but I fear I cannot hold on to it. The moment is critical. As I stand on my toes, my muscles begin to tremble. It is sixty or eighty feet to the precipice. If I lose my hold I shall fall to the bottom, and then perhaps roll over the bench, and tumble still farther down the cliff.

These adventures are genuine; the language is simple enough. Indeed, many explorers and scientists write without fanfare or fireworks. Style is less important than recording the truth.

Powell's accounts of the narrow escapes, his graphic descriptions of the western landscape and its geology read well even today. And the major was by no means alone. Lt. Zebulon Pike (of Pike's Peak fame), Lt. J. J. Ives (the Black Canyon explorer) and many others kept journals. None of them expected these works to be published.

Not all the seafaring or land-exploring journals pack as much excitement as Powell's, of course. Consider Captain James Cook, for instance. While his achievement—a ship's voyage around the world—was important at the time, his record of it could be dry enough. An example:

> *Monday, 5*
>
> Light breezes and Calm all these 24 hours. At 2 p.m. had an Observation of the Sun and moon, which gave the Longitude 8° 42′ W. from Greenwich. At 6 Cape Finister bore S. by W. ½ W., 6 Leagues. Variation of the Compass per Azimuth 18° 42′ W. At Noon, Cape Finister S. by E., distant 4 leagues; lat. observed 43° 4′, therefore Cape Finister must lay in lat. 42° 53′ North. Wind Westerly, N.W., Calm.

The Cook log contained endless pages like this one. Fortunately for the reader, this English captain also left us descriptions of far-flung places and unfamiliar peoples. Here is Cook's encounter with the natives on a small Pacific island in July 1770:

> They were wholy naked, their Skins the Color of Wood soot, and this seem'd to be their Natural Colour. Their Hair was black, lank, and cropt short and neither wooly nor Frizled. Some part of their Bodys had been painted with red, and one of them had his upper lip and breast painted with Streakes of white. Their features were far from being disagreeable; their Voices were soft and Tunable, and they could easily repeat any word after us, but neither us nor Tupia could understand one word they said.

The brave men who pushed toward the North and South Poles kept scientific and personal logbooks. Some of them have stuck in my memory since childhood. What determination these men had! What hardships they had to face! And how bravely they fought their battles against loneliness! Such sufferings in the interest of exploration!

One good example is *Alone*, Admiral Richard E. Byrd's account of his almost five months in Antarctic isolation. On occasion, the admiral's entries describe vistas that seem to be of another planet. Thus:

> . . . Took my daily walk at 4:00 P.M. today, in -89° of frost. The sun had dropped below the horizon, and a blue—of a richness I've never seen anywhere else—flooded in, extinguishing all but the dying embers of the sunset.
>
> Due west, halfway to the zenith, Venus was an unblinking diamond; and opposite her, in the eastern sky, was a brilliant twinkling star set off exquisitely, as was Venus, in the sea of blue. In the northeast a silvergreen serpentine aurora pulsed and quivered gently. In places the Barrier's whiteness had the appearance of dull platinum. It was all delicate and illusive. . . .

Byrd's nightly write-ups would also focus on the terrible chill of the mornings and the difficulties of being alone. ("I'm in a wretched condition.") The admiral's loneliness, his waning strength, and a desolate sense of despair are all conscientiously preserved for posterity.

So are the ordeals and discoveries of other explorers such as Robert Falcon Scott, Roald Amundsen, Ernest Shackelton, Sir Edmund Hillary. The first American Everest expedition during the early 1960s engaged the leading mountain writer of the period, James Ramsey Ullman, to keep a diary.

Naturalists Who Write

Some naturalists of the past were superb writers as well. Think of Henry David Thoreau, for instance, or of John James Audubon. Or consider John Muir, the Californian who explored Yosemite. He wrote eloquently of the storms in the Sierras; he knew the inhabitants of the conifer forests, the history of the rocks, the wildflowers. Muir's writing zeroed in on every detail and on the mood of a place as well. Here is a typical paragraph showing Muir at his best:

> I could distinctly hear the varying tones of individual trees—spruce and fir and pine and leafless oak—and even the infinitely gentle rustle of the withered grasses at my feet. Each was expressing itself in its own way—singing its own song, and making its own peculiar gestures—manifesting a richness of variety to be found in no other forest I have yet seen.

The late Edwin Way Teale, another naturalist, filled sheet after sheet with his descriptions of bird behavior. One day, for instance, Teale charted the minute-by-minute behavior of a bird flock for the duration of forty minutes. And there must have been other such writing since Teale's feat.

Nature lends itself well to the journal.

This becomes especially evident when you read *Pilgrim at Tinker Creek,* a contemporary examination of life around a small waterway. Annie Dillard, the Muir-like author, shines as she tells us about the seasons, about the changing flora and fauna around her creek. She devotes attention to the smallest flying insects, to frogs and puppies. And she writes beautifully about birds. Here is an illustration:

> I walked up to a tree, an Osage orange, and a hundred birds flew away. They simply materialized out of the tree. I saw a tree, then a whisk of color, then a tree again. I walked closer and another hundred blackbirds took flight. Not a branch, not a twig budged: the birds were apparently weightless as well as invisible.
>
> I looked downstream where they flew, and they were gone. Searching, I couldn't spot one. I wandered downstream to force them to play their hand, but they'd crossed the creek and scattered. One show to a customer.

The Diary in the Service of History

In the same vein, much of history comes to us through such chronological accounts. The Greeks, the Romans, and the Egyptians often provided inspiring chronicles. Medieval knights en route to fight in the Holy Land, the romantic men and women of the eighteenth century, the popes, princes, kings, and even their servants left us a legacy of words.

In 1860, for instance, a servant in Napoleon Bonaparte's house carefully wrote down what he heard and saw. An example:

> The Emperor occupied the archiepiscopal palace, a magnificent building situated in a large square on which the grenadiers of the Imperial Guard bivouacked. This bivouac presented a singular scene. Immense kettles, which had been found in the convents, hung, full of mutton, poultry, rabbits, etc., above a fire that was replenished from time to time with furniture, guitars, or mandolins and around which grenadiers, with pipes in their mouths, were

> gravely seated in gilded chairs covered with crimson damask, while they intently watched the kettles as they simmered, and communicated to each other their conjectures on the campaign that had just opened.

And histories of World War I, World War II, the Korean War, and the Vietnam War have been preserved through countless journals of our friends and foes. One such journal was that of Anne Frank, a Jewish teenager whose family tried to hide from the Nazis in Holland. Her diary told about the years of hiding in an Amsterdam attic; it mirrored the young girl's innocence, sweetness, and sensitivity, and her growth between the ages of thirteen and fifteen. Anne's writing ended in August 1944 when the Grüne Polizei made a raid on the "Suret Annexse."Her father, Otto Frank, somehow managed to outlive the Holocaust in Holland, and he wrote about it, too. His daughter Anne died in the Bergen-Belsen concentration camp in March 1945.

The diaries of the Germans themselves provide a clue that Jews were not the only sufferers under Hitler's brutal regime. After World War II, we finally learned about the heroic resistance of six Germans, led by Hans and Sophie Scholl, and their group called the White Rose. All six members were guillotined for their rebellion.

In the meantime, some of the clergy also opposed Hitler. One example was Pastor Martin Niemöeller, who dared to preach from his Berlin pulpit against the Nazis. The courageous Protestant wound up in the Sachenhausen and the Dachau concentration camps. It was during these seven years that Niemöeller wrote some of his most profound wartime journals and sermons. During the same period, other Christian leaders (including many Catholics) suffered immeasurably in various Third Reich prisons. Some of these ministers and priests were to record their physical and emotional sufferings day by sad day in journals that are still with us. Niemöeller was liberated by the Allies but not all of his fellow clerics survived.

A diary also gives us a view of Mussolini's final days. The Italian dictator (who was a one-time journalist) wrote:

> The agony is atrociously long. I'm like the captain of a ship in a storm; the ship is wrecked and I find myself in the churning ocean on a raft that is impossible to guide or govern. No one hears my voice any more.

Mussolini's voice was stilled on April 28, 1945, when he was executed after being caught by partisans near Dongo on Lake Como while he was trying to get to Switzerland.

One can hardly doubt that when it comes to journals, history and politics are twins. Through the centuries, many American presidents felt the need for a public record. John Quincy Adams (1767-1848) and George Washington (1732-1799) come to mind as examples; there are many others. In Europe, British statesmen were long known for writing history in diary form, along with such recent French authors as Camus or Servan-Schreiber. André Gide set down both his early attraction to and his later disenchantment with Russia and communism. In June 1936, after a trip to Moscow, he reflected about the experience:

> There was in my Soviet adventure something tragic. I had arrived there a convinced and enthusiastic

> follower in order to admire a new world, and they offered me, to tempt me and win me, all the prerogatives and privileges that I abhorred in the old world.

And during the years 1938-1940, Gide's disappointment with Marxism found its way almost daily into the author's diary.

Yesteryear's monks and nuns of Europe kept journals that often explored not only their religious beliefs but also the prevailing political situation. The Jesuits of Quebec, Canada, were astute reporters of their times. And more recently, there were luminaries such as Thomas Merton, a Trappist, whose journals are full of wisdom, warmth, spirituality, and political insight. Merton also wrote about his travels, one of which—in Asia—ended his life.

The Travel Journal

"I never travel without my diary. One should always have something sensational to read on the train," joked Oscar Wilde. And throughout time, a multitude of travelers has shared the sights with us.

Some of the most readable travel chronicles are written by adults who possess no literary skills, or by young people who (so far) have not had the time to learn much about writing. Why are some of these diaries so excellent? One reason: the writers were alert; they traveled with their antennas out full tilt, eyes wide open, observing, and making notes.

Age has nothing to do with it. Stephen, a teenage boy from Denver, somehow managed to bounce around the world. Germany. Austria. Turkey. Afghanistan. India. Finally, one day, he alighted near the world's highest mountain chain, the Himalayas.

Moreover, he journeyed into them. Alone. With his note books. And, of course, his journals take in the scene, along with his reactions.

> All around me were the peaks and ridges of Annapurna blazing white, searingly bold. The Himalayas! The Himalayas!
>
> I followed the course of a river up a valley sparkling with deep-blue mountain flowers. I came across the base camps of several trekking expeditions. Giant 26,000-foot Anna purna billowed above it all.
>
> These mountains dazzled one's perceptions. The thin air made one light headed. After resting a little, I trudged upward once more. This time, the face of Annapurna was shining from between heavy cloud folds. The huge mountain reflected the setting sun in one last, victorious hue. An unforgettable Himalayan scene: deeply forested, dark-green silhouettes of other mountains were leaping upward. And still higher, the ice fields.
>
> I marveled at what I saw. It had been worth the effort. I had my reward. I took a photograph and turned back to the village before darkness.

This was written by a youth of seventeen. He captured some of life's elusive moments for always. Wherever he may settle in future, he will be able to savor past sights by just opening his notebooks. He was diligent at writing. Ivan Doig, the novelist from the Northwest, may have spoken for this boy by stating: "A journal must be kept as a ship's log must."

Travel diaries can not only conjure up magic. If they're irreverent enough, the diarists can also make us laugh. Mark Twain was especially good at this. On October 23, 1867, Twain visited Constantinople. His report: "The rustiest old barn . . . . Everywhere dirt, dust, and dinginess . . . ."

The contemporary first-person account often appears in newspapers as well. Some of the writers are people who took a trip, made notes about it, and then sent their chronology to a paper. Travel journals find their way into magazines, too. Sometimes the authors are novices. Yet these diarists already show talent for seeing in colors and shapes, and for the freshness of their language. Sometimes they're blessed by nature with a sense of humor.

Arnold Edinborough, a Canadian journalist and lecturer, decided to keep a diary on a speaking tour through Quebec. His observations later appeared in a Toronto newspaper, the *Financial Post.* Although Edinborough lived it and wrote it more than ten years ago, the material seems as fresh today as if it had been penned yesterday. Here are some excerpts:

> *Monday*
>
> I leave Toronto at noon for Saguenay/Bagotville, the first stop on a two-week speaking tour of Canadian Clubs in Quebec and the Maritimes. Such tours are strenuous.
>
> I arrive on time, but my bag doesn't. No sweat. Ever since I addressed a black-tie banquet in Fredericton one time dressed in a Harris tweed sports jacket with leather patches on the elbows I have traveled dressed in what I am to wear for the meeting. It raises eyebrows on the plane, but it sure saves embarrassment when you get there.
>
> Quebec is still in the grip of dead winter. The snow blows horizontally across the road, whips round the corners of the Manoir and, later in the evening, the wind is rich with the rotten-egg smell of the pulp mill to the south.
>
> The people who live here are the real pioneers of our day. They huddle in the shelter of the great Alcan

smelter—their township a mere dot on the bleak granite of the Canadian shield.

Tuesday

A bus takes me very early from Shawinigan to Trois-Rivières, and I have a longish wait in the CP Rail station there. It is a cavernous place. This morning there are very few people, and the straight rows of dark hard seats in the waiting room look like an empty church.

The pictures on the walls are heroic in both size and subject, and there is a series of armorial bearings of great French explorers and settlers.

I am the only person in the parlor car to Montreal and, when I start to write this diary on my knee, the trainman bustles about to set me up with a table. A steward brings me coffee, offers me a cigarette, and addresses me as "Mon ami." It's still a great way to travel, especially since my bag is in the rack above.

Wednesday

To St. Andrews-by-the-Sea for the weekend. "You'll be quiet anyway," says the taxidriver. "They take the sidewalks up in September there and don't put 'em out again until May."

He's almost right. Walk out on the jetty two hundred yards, walk left one hundred from the hotel and right four hundred—that's it.

Preserving Your Family Heritage via a Diary

A travel diary can also stick to the bare bones; it may just mention where a family spent a vacation five years ago—or last year, for that matter. The bare facts—day of departure, mode of travel, accommodations, activities—can come in handy when you decide on future vacations. Besides, the journal brings back happy memories that hold a family together.

The chronicle of a marriage could start from the very beginning with wedding preparations, the wedding itself, the honeymoon, and so on. These milestones all fit into a bound book. The diary can be written in the "we" form. It can later concentrate on the important dates—wedding anniversaries, births of children, job transfers, moves, professional achievements, awards. The book will serve your children in their adult years. Memorabilia. Nostalgia.

I recently read such a family diary written by a Pennsylvania woman who was concerned about the leaking Harrisburg nuclear plant because she was pregnant. Her husband, meanwhile, had taken on a new job. This added both suspense and stress to the diary. Her visits to the doctor and the family's preparation for a natural childbirth all quickened the pace of the entries.

Childbirth and the week-by-week observation of a growing youngster are certainly worth recording. What a priceless document, that chronicle of your children growing up! Indeed, I feel a pang of emotion today—twenty years later—when I reread my old family diaries. I'd faithfully kept track of my impressions and sensations right from the beginning of these new lives.

For instance: What was it like to hold a small baby in your arms? How did it react to the world around? Which were the first spoken words? How did the siblings deal with one another? What happened during family outings? And what were the signs of a child's maturing?

I kept an especially detailed book about my youngest son after it became clear that we would have no more children. Niccolo had spent just two days in this world when I wrote: "Niccolo is tiny but exquisitely complete: miniature hands and feet. Small but already expressive face—pink but not red or raw." And after five days when the infant is home: "We feel his sudden magnetic presence in the house; must look at him again and again." After two weeks: "He begins to notice the narrow borders of his universe—the blanket, perhaps, or the polka dots of his crib." And after five weeks, there appears this entry:

> Future Outdoorsman, we call him as he sleeps in the shade of our oak tree. He snoozes in his little plastic crib—his cheeks rosy, minihands clenched. When he awakens, a word will make him smile—surprisingly, dazzlingly—giving, oh, so much pleasure!

Upon rereading this, two decades later, my spine tingles with pleasure.

To be sure, such a chronicle should follow your offspring through many weeks. After four months, I write:

> Energy! Initiative! Curiosity! While on his tummy, Niccolo now lifts his head. He studies the world out of large, blond-lashed, gray-blue eyes. It's an effort, coming up like this. His mother calls the craning pink head a rising moon. Niccolo's voice is now capable of variations: squeaks of contentment, for instance, or angry little outbursts in high notes—where's my milk?

After eight months, I wrote:

> He crawls! His elbows dig into the grass and forward he goes! Try to stop him! He will only cackle and giggle and laugh. He is no longer afraid and must touch everything. His *joie de vivre* seems infectious. He makes us all happy . . . .

Not all family chronicles are this joyful; the river of life flows unevenly; there are the gentle stretches but also the rapids. Families suffer ups and downs. You may know a father who, while witnessing a childbirth, got butterflies in his stomach and couldn't stay for the entire momentous event. A New England mother kept a diary about her severely handicapped child. And an older man dictated a description of his painful struggles and his helplessness after suffering a stroke.

There is much to be said for such diaries. Anne Morrow Lindbergh may have expressed it best. "I must write it all out, at any cost. Writing is thinking. It is more than living, for it is being conscious of living."

In the next chapter we'll see what psychiatrists and psychologists have to say on the subject.

4

The Diary: What Psychiatrists and Psychologists Say

The Journal as a Release

Keeping a diary really proves its worth when we're suddenly face to face with a crisis.

A middle-aged man learns that he has a grave illness. He overcomes his fears and regains some of his balance by starting a journal.

A young girl loses a boyfriend who had still sworn his love to her a few days before. Inconsolable at first, she eventually eases her anguish by writing about it.

A woman who never married realizes one morning that she has no one in her life. No close friends. No family. No one at all. She weathers this discovery by communicating with her new journal.

Behavioral scientists know how major stresses—the departure or absence of love, a terminal illness, the loss of a much-needed job, even menopause—can temporarily derail us. But many mental-health practitioners offer a remedy. Emoting on paper can bring relief.

These days, psychologists encourage crisis-facing males to let go of their emotions, to release their anguish and fears and inner torments, and even to cry. You might compare the release mechanism to a session with a psychiatrist whose quiet empathy helps you to start talking. You talk it all out, which makes you feel better. Dr. Sidney Werkman, a psychiatrist who has done important work in the field of stress, says that the diary-writer can let go by letting it "flow" via stream-of-consciousness writing. This means that you can write anything and move even from subject to subject until your thoughts veer to the problems in your life.

A failing marriage is one of the major crisis themes in adult journals. The anxiety and stress generated by marital failure urgently demand a release. Your diary is a good listener. Already in 1862, while struggling with (and depressed by) a bad marriage, Countess Tolstoy took to her journal.

One modern husband, a midwesterner, reaches for the same outlet as he faces a painful situation with his long-time spouse. He does not spare himself. He writes:

> At dinner, she finally admits it: she doesn't love me! Oh, I already knew this. But at last—at last—after ten years of marriage, it is out in the open! She finally summoned the courage to put it into words!

The man records some of his wife's statements:

> She feels some comradeship occasionally, she admits, ah, yes, and pity, too, once in awhile for both of us, she says. But no love. I decide to sleep in my study; this way I won't be tempted to admit that I still love her. And she won't have to fear my night-time

> embrace, which she always repulses. God only knows how much I want to hold her in my arms—

The experts tell us that the intensity of emotion and reality of the diary entries can help this man, alleviating pain, and in time setting him on the road to recovery. Dr. Werkman, the Denver psychiatrist, calls such journal writing a *cri de coeur*, a cry of the heart. It eventually brings inner peace.

One such *cri* comes from a forty-year-old New Yorker mated to the wrong woman. His description of her is one-sided, but at least he gets a lingering discontent off his chest. He spews it out with some anger:

> She is unbelievably irritable and discourteous toward me. Maybe she is nasty on purpose because she wants to hurt me. But why, oh, why? She has no friends. Despite her sharp intelligence, she doesn't seem to attract or hold people. Perhaps they suspect her snobbishness; perhaps they're repulsed by her brashness. She's loud, yet lacking assurance and poise. She hides from people, hides from the telephone, hides from social obligations (adult parties are a scourge to her). She sees no connection between entertaining people and my professional advancement, makes no effort to help me on the way up.
>
> Why am I still with her? Is it love? Or the cowardice of ending a marriage?

Another husband lessened the separation stresses by journal-writing. Later, the couple meet for a family breakfast at Easter. Almost at once, things go badly. To the man's surprise and overt disappointment, his daughter isn't there. He immediately blames his estranged wife for keeping the daughter away. When the two adults go for an after-breakfast walk, a verbal fight erupts.

The couple try for a get-together a few weeks later. But the marriage seems a lost cause.

The husband describes it graphically:

> *December 14*
>
> The fight begins again, and our words smack back and forth like bullets. Silence, reloading, bang. Silence, reloading, bang. My wife is unbelievably bitter. She thinks I cheated on her while she was at the hospital for the hysterectomy. I did not cheat on her! So far, I've always been faithful. Yet she burns with unwarranted jealousy. She wakes me up at 4:00 in the morning, Gestapo-style. And tries to grill me! Had I gone out at night? Did I visit other women? She tears me out of the bed at 6:00 A.M. again, her machine guns of bitterness at the ready. Why must she always deprive me of sleep?
>
> Of course, she hasn't slept, either. She hasn't even eaten for twenty-four hours . . . .

Dr. Werkman considers such anguished entries an emotional safety valve and stress-reducer. Moreover, by rereading his diary, the husband can confront his position. Eventually, he understands that the marriage was over. Writing it all down reduced much of his pain and his grief.

One of Dr. Werkman's colleagues agrees. "The diary is a valid way to come to grips with a problem," says Dr. John G. Young, a veteran's hospital psychiatrist and director of the Center for Creativity. Dr. Young recommends that journal-writing be honest, however. "The writer must focus on *feelings*," says Dr. Young. "And the diary can help bring these feelings to the surface."

Many psychotherapists welcome diary-writing for individuals who are comfortable with the medium and willing to communicate. "I certainly do believe in the value of diaries," Dr. Rollo May commented in response to my query. Some Japanese psychiatrists suggest that their patients reach for pen and paper also. A similar view is represented by a well-known Pennsylvania psychiatric outpatient clinic.

Moreover, Dr. Ira Progoff, a psychologist and one of the most respected specialists in this field, already had begun to use the journal as an outlet in 1957, along with psychotherapy. "It had a favorable effect therapeutically," writes Dr. Progoff. "So I extended the procedure." More on his methods later.

Many therapists themselves reach for their diaries in a crisis. One example is the late Dr. Fritz Perls. One day he learned that his young wife suffered from incurable leukemia; as she slowly began to die, his own anguish and sadness sent him to his journal. The latter became a receptacle to cope with the grief caused by her eventual death. Such grief is often associated with anger as well, and one can release this anger by writing about it. The diary can thus become crucial in the mourning process; a helpmate in working it through and getting going again.

Death is indeed a frequent subject. Here, a man touchingly remembers a trip with his fiancée, who later died:

> We worked for a few days in the French vineyards and watched a bicycle race in a small French town and held our breaths in the Strasbourg cathedral.
>
> In a small Bourgogne town, we came upon a country cemetery; it slanted uphill toward a château. The gravestones were two to three hundred years old.
>
> We studied the inscriptions. One of the stones held our attention. It showed the picture of a girl and the words, *Nos yeux no cessaient pas de pleurer apres les*

tiennes se fermaient—"Our eyes never stopped crying after yours had closed."

I cry a great deal, and some of my tears are inward.

The Diary's Role as a Friend

In recent years, psychotherapists have begun to emphasize the importance of liking yourself before you can love someone else. "To activate love in your life, you first have to turn within," says Dr. Ken Wydra. "In a certain way, you first have to fall in love with yourself." Many other psychologists hold the same position.

To be sure, the diary can become a useful tool in making friends with yourself.

Indeed, how long has it been since we examined our own character traits? How long has it been since we sat down to make a list of our kind deeds? Or catalogued our recent achievements?

A journal, say the experts, can help improve a person's self-image. Out of it may grow a new self-esteem, or self-worth, or at least a sense of significance in this big world. The journal thereby becomes our most devoted, most patient friend. This is all the more true when intimacy with others has become difficult to achieve; even our best friends may rush too much. They're engaged in their own survival battles, their own searches. They're a little too busy, too harassed for intimacy. Dr. Rollo May expressed it well, this demise of closeness between human beings. "In our day," he writes, "it is a common practice to avoid working up the courage required for authentic intimacy." And Dr. George Bach, another psychiatrist, describes the aftermath of the dating bar, the singles meeting, telling us that "everyone goes home, if not empty-handed then at least empty-hearted, feeling a little more lonely, a little more hopeless. . . ."

An intimate diary changes this situation altogether. You can pour your true feelings and thoughts into the pages. You become intimate with yourself.

Dr. Werkman suggests that you write spontaneously. Don't hold back. If you let your emotions go, the words will not fail you. They may come in torrents. In time, this pouring-out-of-it-all becomes so satisfying that your diary-writing gains momentum. And as you make friends with yourself, you'll be stronger for it. In the future, not much can faze you or derail you again.

Gaining Access to the Self

"There is so little time," says Dr. Werkman. "Many of us hurry through life. We must stop for contemplation!" According to this psychiatrist, contemplation—via a diary—"helps you get in touch with yourself." A former secretary-general of the United Nations, Dag Hammarskjold, who kept a journal for many years, called it "a sort of white book concerning the negotiations with myself—and God." And May Sarton said it helped her "open the door into the subconscious." In short, the diary aids in gaining access to the self.

Such looking inward can be scary at first for some people. As we noted, Americans are accustomed to masking their real feelings in public. Showing emotions outwardly is taboo, so it follows that many individuals don't want to look under their own surfaces either. Such self-analysis might rock the emotional boat. Self-confrontation may show up some problems. Yet according to the most knowledgeable mental health workers—Dr. Rollo May, for instance—the opposite is true. "The more self-awareness a person has, the more alive he or she is," explains Dr. May, who has no objection to your achieving that awareness by means of a diary.

The diary becomes a data bank. It gives you a chance to take your own emotional temperature, to assess your moods. One writer calls it a "reaching into the recesses of your mind—a voyage into the interior."

The voyage should be made with open eyes. Sincerity is needed for this exploration. An artist, for instance, discovers that he/she has self-doubts; by admitting these to himself or herself, he or she eventually defeats them. Dr. Werkman puts it this way: "Self-awareness makes a problem coherent." May Sarton realized one October day that she could not always believe in her own work but that even the failures were meaningful. Sarton suddenly saw the silver linings in her life. She told her diary:

> The fact that a middle-aged, single woman, without any vestige of family left, lives in this house in a silent village and is responsible only to her own soul means something. The fact that she is a writer and can tell where she is and what it is like on the pilgrimage inward can be of comfort.

For other writers, the situation is not as clear. But at least they muster the honesty to set down their thoughts. They may not always succeed. But at least they make an effort to understand themselves. One middle-aged author explores some moments of trepidation:

April 2

Sudden doubts. My ancient phonograph plays the haunting Grieg "Symphonic Dances." I feel melancholy. Is it just age? The effect of a thirty-minute sauna? I don't know.

There's little reason to complain. Lots of trips coming up. Good health. A devoted (but introverted) womanfriend who tries to be good company. Last Christmas, we listened to a church choir; two weeks ago, it was an evening at the Metropolitan Opera on the new, color TV set. We see most of the important new movies. We ski cross-country and Alpine. We hike all summer. She's reliable and caring although not exactly effusive. I should be happy. Something is amiss, though, I don't know what it is.

Toward Growth

Such probing eventually turns up an answer. What's more, we can also bring to light how we feel toward others, including those who are closest to us. How do we really get along with our spouses, our lovers, our children? Where do we stand in our most important relationships? Dr. George Bach recommends that we reflect upon this at regular intervals. He calls it a state-of-the-union message and advises that we share the message with our partner. Openly. Directly. Dr. Bach explains: "We encourage pairs to ask at regular intervals, 'Where are we now?' and to answer honestly. Such encounters make sudden reversals unlikely. The state-of-the-union message keeps a relationship up-to-date. . . ."

Such stocktaking can be done first via your journal. The advantage? You can weigh the situation. You can choose your words fairly. When you finally come face-to-face with your partner to deliver "the message," you will make more sense.

Unfortunately, not all such messages are positive ones. On occasion, life forces us to terminate a chronically ailing relationship so as to be free for a healthier one. One example comes from the pen of a wife who, after sixteen years of marriage and several sessions with a psychologist, reaches the conclusion that things must change soon. She writes:

> We both know that there can't be many more crises. We'll have to decide one way or another soon. We're both forty; if we split now, we'd both have the time to find true happiness with someone else. I must convince him that we're better off apart. I assume that he will welcome a separation. . . .

This diary entry helped this woman toward clarity and freedom. A husband in a similar dilemma used his diary to quell his inner turmoil. The years of writing down his hurts eventually healed him, too. He didn't use his notes for decision-making; in fact, he never opened the journals of all those many hurtful years. It was only when he was finally separated, and ready for a new life, that he dared to reread his old diaries.

The entries proved to be an eye-opening boon. The frustrations of the past became clear. He suddenly understood that he had put the years of insoluble conflict behind him. Right there, that evening, the diary helped this individual to jettison a painful past. He felt no bitterness at all; he was simply rid of the bygone.

He had grown. He had changed. He was eager for a better life. Anaïs Nin once expressed it well. A diary, she felt, reduced the past to "an adventure and a tale, to a story of a life. . . ."

Such rereadings often bring moments that are buoyant with hope and fresh viewpoints. In *Recovering: A Journal 1978-79,* May Sarton realizes one October day that she is on a rising curve. She contemplates this development:

> What has changed in a miraculous way is the landscape of the heart, so somber and tormented for over a year that I was not myself. . . . What has happened, that quite suddenly some weeks ago the landscape became luminous and peaceful, no anger, no irritation, as though the screen that had separated us for so long had simply lifted away as fog sometimes does in these parts? Whatever the cause, it feels like a miracle.

She welcomes "joy and praise back," as she puts it.

The reexamination of our diaries provides an opportunity to observe our gradual maturing. What wondrous change!

It might have begun in A.D. 397 when Saint Augustine began to confess his sins in writing. On page after page, the future theologian accused himself of his skepticism toward the Scriptures, of falling in "with a set of sensualists who had the snares of the devil in their mouths." He even confessed to stealing pears (which he threw to the pigs).

Step by step, we follow a discovery of his spiritual growth. "Can any praise be worthy of the Lord's Majesty?" he writes after conversion. "How magnificent his strength! How inscrutable his wisdom!" And after his baptism in A.D. 387, he fervently embraces the Scriptures. St. Augustine's sincerity and passion make his *Confessions* still remarkable. From sinner to saint!

Our own development can hardly match such Christian drama, yet may be no less satisfying. For instance: A fifty-six-year-old man looks back at the diaries of his thirties to discover that he was once a very angry man. What rages! How quickly he would explode! His current journal entries show him that he handles people much better now. He has achieved self-control. He has mellowed as a person. This realization must have made him feel good indeed.

Reviewing our journals can help us pinpoint some patterns that should be broken—a repeated unkindness toward someone, for instance, or a lack of forgiveness. Recognizing such things may set the reader onto the route of change. To be sure, a study of diary pages over a long period must surely bring understanding of the self. Questions and answers fall into place. For instance: Has my self-confidence improved through the months or years? Or am I still somewhat shy or inhibited? Do the entries show that I've become more patient? Or am I curt with people? Am I still somewhat high-strung? Or more on an even keel? Did I suffer from certain phobias that I've now overcome? Do I presently see the good in people, or have I become cynical about others? Is there a problem that still needs to be solved, a life situation that must be ameliorated? Dr. Progoff, the therapist who specializes in national diary workshops, suggests that you also reread your journal with an eye to your physical state. It's true that your notes could help a physician who will some day examine you. But Dr. Progoff goes a step further. He asks: "Can you connect any frequent references to physical ailments (headaches, stomachaches) with some recurrent emotional state?"

The Diary as Indicator of Whether or Not You Need Help

Psychiatrists and psychologists insist that there are limits to the benefits of diary-writing. Some human dilemmas and some crises can be so overpowering that a million written words and months of self-analysis won't make a dent in your psyche. You *still* can't function well. You still sleep badly. You still have trouble going to work.

In such cases, the individual must seek outside help. It may come from a priest, minister, or rabbi, or from some other experienced counselor. Dr. Sidney Werkman, the psychiatrist, feels that if a crisis, depression, or other problem has not cleared up in about four weeks, it is time to get assistance. There might be danger signals. Compulsive drinking, for instance, or chronic drug use, thoughts of suicide, and other mental health problems. The counselor may encourage you to continue journal-writing.

Journal Workshops

For individuals who see a merit in journal-writing but would prefer to do it in a structured class, the solution is a Progoff Intensive Workshop. It is the creation of Dr. Ira Progoff, a New York psychologist who started his workshops during the mid-sixties. Since then, he has integrated journal-writing into a well-honed, well-organized, psychological self-aid program.

Progoff's journal workshop retreats take place all

over the United States and Canada, often with the blessing of theology schools and churches. Progoff's self-published books have been bestsellers. And his theories are widely accepted by both psychiatrists and the clergy. Unlike ordinary diaries, which you can write as you please, Progoff's National Intensive Journal Program uses a special loose-leaf format: Your diary is divided into numerous sections, each with a different purpose. Some sections come with elegant labels such as "Twilight Imagery Log" or the "Inner Wisdom Dialogue." Other sections focus on your body, your relationships, your life history. Dr. Progoff's program goes deeper than you would go on your own; like a psychiatrist, he allows you to return all the way to your childhood.

During the workshops, you're engaged to explore many facets of your life. You don't have to share your notes with others in the class. But you may do so if you wish, and read excerpts aloud. Dr. Progoff, like all diarists, knows the benefits of writing: the crystallization of your ideas, a clearer perception of the world around you, the summoning of inner resources. In short, this is a journal program with an expert teacher at your elbow.

Some of your classmates may have come because they're in a personal crisis, or "at a time of transition," to use Dr. Progoff's words. But many other students are people *without* major problems. You begin with a "Life Context Workshop," followed by the "Depth Feedback Workshop" and the "Process Meditation Workshop." Some of the Progoff programs fit into a marathon weekend. Some are taught by his trained leaders. Dr. Progoff's textbook is listed in the bibliography on page 144.

Dreams and Your Diary

One of Dr. Progoff's sessions concerns your dreams; his "Dream Log" is for "describing them just as you recall them."

Dreams have long fascinated psychotherapists and diarists alike; they pop up in all the important journals, from André Gide's to May Sarton's. And, of course, dreams have no relationship to the future; they're not predictions at all and seldom come true. Instead, they're pieces of subconscious flotsam and jetsam that wash into your sleep; when you awaken you can't always remember them. Psychiatrists say that dreams are "the language of your unconscious" and therefore set great store by them; dreams certainly express our (often secret) wishes and our (not so secret) fears. (Illustration for the latter: Sarton once dreamed that, during an absence, her house had been ransacked.)

Freud wrote volumes about dreams. He attached all kinds of symbolism to various images: a bird in flight, for instance, expressed sexual desire. And a departure symbolized death. Dr. Progoff takes a somewhat more pragmatic view. He writes that "dreams reflect the tensions and anxieties that are bound to arise in a person's life out of the conflict between immediate desires and the requirements of the long-range goals of one's life. Many of these conflicts are not conscious to the individual, but the dreams express them and carry them further toward resolution."

Dreams give free rein to our imagination. My son Stephen, for instance, while far away on the Mediterranean island of Crete at age nineteen, recorded the following dream in his diary:

> In a half delirium, this dark, briny morn, I dreamed I was in Jan's car. She had suggested going to a party that evening. I wanted to tell her that I would rather have gone to her place and made love to her. Suddenly the alarm clock shatters my dream. The room is a giant sea shell. All I can hear between my hacking and writing is the bellicose sea.

The Cretan sea shell setting fits. And a nineteen-year-old is bound to miss his girl-friend.

Rollo May claims that even "the unskilled person may get occasional useful guidance from dreams, and even insights into solutions of problems." Dr. Sidney Werkman, meanwhile, asserts that dream interpretation is not easy for the layperson. But with talent and application, it can be learned.

The diary proves its value in this respect, too. The diarist can pinpoint dreams as the scientist pinpoints a butterfly.

The Diary and Your Handwriting

When it comes to analytical tools, one final possibility should be mentioned—an examination of your handwriting. Graphology is taken seriously in Europe, where psychiatrists and psychologists use it as an adjunct to treatment.

If you have enough motivation, handwriting analysis is not difficult to learn. Some colleges nowadays include graphology in their curriculums. And there are some up-to-date, easy-to-understand books on the subject. (One of them is *The Graphology Handbook,* published by Para-Research and listed in the bibliography.)

Graphology can tell you much about your own development; the overall picture of your script points to inner harmony and balance. Exaggerations in a handwriting and sudden directional shifts reveal that the writer has some problems. Skilled analysts can even detect severe mental or physical illness. And a comparison between how you wrote five years ago (or longer) and the way you write now can tell much about your current state of mind. To analyze correctly, however, requires not only dedicated study but experience as well. No expert ever fell from the graphological heavens.

In Europe, this science is used even to evaluate someone's professional aptitude or to determine how a person would get along with another person. In such cases, both scripts are examined.

One final word of caution. Graphology has nothing to do with "Grapho-Analysis." The latter is taught quickly to anyone willing to spend nine hundred dollars for a correspondence course. Grapho-Analysis, while popular in the United States, leans mostly on trivia, such as the crossing of *t*'s or the dotting of *i*'s. Graphology goes much deeper and further.

5

The Diary and the Author

An Exercise for New Authors

Judging from the popularity—and circulation—of America's magazines for writers, every American apparently wants to write. For fame. For money. For self-expression. To influence others.

How do you begin, then? With a poem? A short letter to a newspaper editor? A short short story?

All good. But the diary is another way to get started. I often ask my adult students in creative writing classes during the first session: Has anyone here kept a diary? Regularly? A few hands shoot up. I sincerely applaud these scribes. It's a good sign, that journal-writing, just as voluminous love letters are a good sign. These people *are* writers; they need to express themselves.

The budding wordsmith should go to it. The diary helps you to become more nimble with pen or typewriter. You make a start at threading words and sentences into a coherent weave. The journal is a prelude to an essay (it may also be the other way around), or to your first short article.

Such "private" writing gives you practice. After all, there are only rare geniuses who can immediately turn out a good short story or a novel or a superior nonfiction book. Trial and error first! Even the flexing of emotional and intellectual muscles requires practice.

Future book critics can sharpen their language here, in private, away from the limelight of the magazine or newspaper column. Prospective movie reviewers can test their mettle with an outrageously honest critique that would find few takers in the real newspaper or magazine world. Budding political columnists, emerging exposé writers, and incorruptible travel reporters can refine their ideas and biases in their own journals.

Diary-writing offers the greatest of freedoms. It is much more joyful than commercial writing for slick magazines. The diarist need please only himself or herself, and not the market. As you make your entries, you do so for your own gratification. No compromises. Audience of one. (Future assignments will change all that; most working press editors—and the editors of commercial magazines—are conformists by force. They will generally expect you to say what the public wants to hear, or they won't print your stuff.)

As a diarist, you can say what *you* like:

> *Stapleton International, Denver* *4* P.M., *April 14*
> Flight #368 to Boston. I'm punctual; the jet is not. It arrives 45 minutes late in Denver. There are 150 of us who want to board. Only one agent at the counter. He explains cooly, without apology, that there will be

> a 30-minute delay. One of the plane's instruments is on the blink. We wait for an hour. Then we're told that another Boston flight leaves at Gate Number so and so. I *schlepp* my portable typewriter and heavy paper-laden suitcase to the gate. Here a ticket agent tells us that this jet leaves for Seattle, not Boston. We're reshuffled two more times until—at last—we board the flight to our destination. Two hours lost. Late night arrival on the east coast . . . .

This is an actual diary entry. Unpublished, of course. No sane newspaper editor would print this. Much too critical. Working press editors are afraid of their publishers, who live in fear of their major advertisers (in this case, an airline). As a result, and in most instances, travel writers say nice things. Some of their writings read almost like travel brochures.

On the other hand, a diary can have realism in its favor. You see, your diary can't reject you. (E. J. Kahn, a *New Yorker* writer, once compared his journal to "a patient retriever.")

In short, I "published" my airline experience in my patient journal. In fact, I wrote it on the plane, on the carrier's in-flight stationery, and later pasted it in my journal.

The diary is the professional author's storage bin of ideas, facts, observations, true-life impressions. Many great names—from Graham Greene to the late John Steinbeck to poet James Dickey and dozens more—have collected materials this way. John M. Allen, a highly placed editor and executive of the *Reader's Digest,* comments: "I think every writer—any writer worth his salt—keeps a journal, jotting down not so much what happened, but how things looked, felt, smelled, etc. It not only enhances the writing ability, but it also enhances the living ability, the ability to observe, to appreciate, to use the senses."

For many professional writers, the diary simply feeds their habits; genuine writers must write just as singers must sing and concert pianists must play the piano. A compulsion, perhaps. Moreover, diaries and other writing forms share a symbiotic relationship, growing out of one another.

In an interview, Anaïs Nin, said: "By writing the diaries I was exercising my art and disciplining myself, which helped me in the novels, and the novels reinforced the diaries."

The Diarist/Fictioneer

Nin was no exception, what with diaries supporting novels and vice versa. Howard Nemerov, May Sarton, James Dickey, John Dos Passos, André Gide, and Georges Simenon are a few of the many others who found that the two disciplines complement each other. Alexandr Solzhenitsyn's extraordinary descriptive powers first surfaced in his diary notes, which led, indirectly, to a Nobel Prize. Steinbeck's autobiographical *Travels with Charley* started in this manner. Kafka was a hard-working diarist. And Mark Twain was a witty one. Most literary lions (or lionesses) are notoriously powerful journal writers.

But what of the *new* fictioneer? He/She would be wise to grab those white pages and fill them with ideas for short stories or novels. Let the diary become the sketchpad for some human portraits or, if you're up to it, some ambitious characterizations and personal reflections. A young American suns himself on the white-washed roof of a little rented house in St.

Julian's, Malta. Suddenly, he begins to ponder about death. Thus:

> Sprawled nude in the sun this afternoon, I savored sublime transcience. "Life," I sighed, adding with only a trace of sorrow, "Soon, too soon I will lose it." The death sentiment often steals through the canals of my brain. I do not believe that there is anything a living thing can do to alter the eventual demise. I'm likely to view a brief respite in eternity. Resolution: I must expose my life to as much as I can emotionally, physically, and mentally. I must continually seek to enlarge my domain of experience.

A few days later, on the same roof, the young author reread these lines and began to fashion a short story from the raw material they provided.

Fiction writers know that all short stories and novels start as seeds that can fit into a journal, where they can germinate, to grow into scenes, plots, complete stories or books. Example? Theodor Plievier, a German novelist, once read Homer's *Iliad.* The seed was a single sentence that caught the German author's eyes. *The chance of war is equal; the slayer oft is slain!* So Homer. In time, Plievier wrote a shattering World War II novel with the same theme.

Some authors find other employment for their journals: they may designate them as actual workbooks for developing novels. Example? When I began to create *The Peacemakers,* a fictional work that dealt with a future General Patton type, I filled my diary with a hail of notes. Notes about my characters, specifically about how this macho general talked. I wrote:

> Said fanatically; he accused; he added; bullied;

> cracked; cut in; roared; thundered; said in his barrack-square tone. He bellowed.

A day later, I sat down for a long session to imagine and catalogue the general's gestures:

> Pounds his chest—takes drag at beer.
> General's arm boxed the air in front of.
> Looped thumb under belt.
> Crossed his arms in front of him.
> Good mood—slaps people on back.
> Wipes mouth with back of hand.
> Smacks his fist into his palm.
> Makes brusque motions with neck.
> Takes hungry drag from cigarette—flicks ashes on floor.
> Wets forefinger as he turns pages.
>
> And his motivations: *He wants to fight. Wants to function as a general. Wants fame.*

It is intriguing to note that a professional writer's diary seems to focus on other people, on surroundings, and on the times. There seldom is any narcissism. The better the author, of course, the better, the more compelling the images, the descriptions. A Steinbeck, a Nabokov, a Greene, or a Sarton can write so superbly that even a brief diary entry or letter may sound like an excerpt from a novel. Andre Gide actually put down snatches of dialogue; in one case, he re-created a conversation between two very old men. The diary dialogue becomes as real as life itself. So are his descriptions of the French Riviera, Corsica, Paris, Rome, Naples, and other locales. Gide also enlisted his journals for setting down many pointed complaints about the critics of his novels. The diaries of great writers contain rich details that add up to a lavishly wrought tapestry.

The "Business" of Diary Writing

Of course, we must not forget that there have always been diarists who make the diaries their business. Anaïs Nin's six-volume output is one example; it led to fame and fortune and prominence for this woman. At the end, before her death from cancer, there was a Nin cult. She lectured all over the world. She received an avalanche of mail. The letters came mostly from women who adored her, who claimed that her diaries had changed their lives. By contrast, one recent reviewer called Nin's writings "little more than a long tease, a fluttering of veils. . . ." May Sarton's journals were always more serious and brought in much less money, a fact that *can* signal quality. Katherine Mansfield, the fine short story writer, was a solid diarist as well. And one cannot fault Simone de Beauvoir, a Frenchwoman and confidante of Sartre.

During the early eighties, novelist Ivan Doig made a name for himself by combining the logbook of James G. Swan, a nineteenth-century pioneer in the Pacific Northwest, with his own diary. Doig follows Swan's many journeys and fuses the two journals in a literary tour de force.

I don't know who said, "Always keep a diary. Some day it may keep you!" It is certainly good advice for those artisans with words, the professional writers.

Magazine and Newspaper Diaries

Naturally, a short diary is also suitable for a magazine or a newspaper; a writer may favor the chronological form to depict a political event, a personal nightmare, the story of a conversion. Moreover, the form works well in the adventure or travel fields. A young woman, for instance, describes her day-by-day trials during a white-river expedition; this raft story is published in *Cosmopolitan* magazine. A young Canadian reporter uses the diary form (Sunday, Monday, etc.) for a blow-by-blow account of his good times at a far-flung Club Med vacation village; a slick Canadian airline magazine publishes it. Another travel writer sells an account of a Sunday-to-Saturday vacation in the Bahamas, complete with her personal reactions. The use of day names sans dates makes such writing a little more timeless.

Here is a typical excerpt from one of my cruise diaries. Note the friendly, uncritical tone:

> *Saturday*
>
> It is icy in Chicago, smoggy in Los Angeles. We sail at 9:00 P.M. bound for the sun of Puerto Vallarta, Acapulco, Mazatlán. I stand at the ship's rail, alone, wondering how it will go this time. Will cruising again mean the proverbial feast-at-sea, the floating superresort? Will it give health and the Fountain of Youth? That depends on the cruise ship and on the passengers.
>
> They're still coming aboard, many of them looking pale, a bit pinched, ready for the Total Vacation. It has begun well enough: white-smocked men take the suitcases to the cabins. I begin to explore what will be my hotel for the next eleven days. Many stateroom doors are open and I see champagne bottles, trays of hors d'oeuvres, excited faces. The public rooms buzz with more islands of partying groups. It is difficult to know who's who, to distinguish visitors from passengers. On the deck below us, bright klieg lights concentrate on our ship's white hull and on the immaculate decks; a movie crew is setting up their cameras. From the portside, some people already toss garlands of confetti. Almost everyone holds a glass in hand.

This must be the fifteenth big liner I have traveled on, but always, I feel a strong sense of suspense. A cruise is much better than the normal ocean voyage. A cruise means ports of call, new sights, land possibilities, the geography lesson, and the extra luxury rolled into one.

"All visitors ashore, please!" is repeated at intervals of fifteen minutes, first in English, then in Italian because our ship is of Italian registry. At last, I hear the deep, bellowing blasts from the smokestacks. "Come to sea, come to sea," the ship calls. One of the orchestras plays on the sun deck, but the music is lost among the yells of bon voyage. We're in motion. I look at my watch. 9:00 P.M. Punctual.

Almost at once, the upper decks start to empty, and I know the reason; the dining-room doors have opened, and some three hundred people—almost everyone—line up for the welcoming buffet. It seems to pop out of the brochures. I pay homage to pink-jellied salmons, adorned with mayonnaise shaped like flowers, to mountains of white shrimp, red lobsters, dark-brown smoked hams, Tabasco-colored salami, to large beef roasts, broiled chickens, forty salads and vegetables, twenty kinds of pasta, an array of pastries and petits fours.

Sunday

Our vessel carries some substantial passengers. There is B.F., a well-known MGM producer, who looks like the popular notion of a producer, a very solid man, but kind. There's A.B., a noted playwright, who plays table tennis like a champion. In time, I get to know a director of documentary films, an ABC-TV cameraman who's been around the world ten times, various TV actors, and a fellow who decorates Hearst homes. I also meet a Los Angeles lady who keeps calling Mazatlán "Matzoball." And a woman from Pasadena who brought aboard—I can hardly believe it until I see it—a jar of peanut butter. Our dining-room table consists of only one other man, a San Francisco attorney with excellent manners. The rest are four widows in their fifties and sixties. One of the widows owns an elegant Beverly Hills dress shop. Another, a trim, bright person, inherited a wholesale food company. She's from Joliet, Illinois, and she seems to possess a good business sense. Our waiter's name is Dino, and he likes to clown.

Monday

We see nothing but the ocean, which now ripples like silver, then changes to dark-blue ink, then turns as green as the eyes of a Persian cat. I watch the water from a deck chair. In the morning, we had our "Fire and Boat" drill, with everyone looking droll in the orange-colored life preservers. The captain gave orders to lower the lifeboats. The machinery worked.

By now, we've taken stock of our 12,210-ton ship. She is less than 500 feet long and only 70 feet wide. She was built in Trieste. The cabins contain small, red telephones; if someone rings you, the phone sings like a canary. You also get closed circuit television and piped-in music. A buzzer brings your cabin steward at all hours. This isn't a ship to get lost on. The decks are arranged with great simplicity, and I get a feeling of good design throughout.

Six P.M. I'm back on the deck chair. A strip of land—Baja, California—melts with the darkness. No lights. This portion of the coast is not inhabited. A wind is coming up, and before checking on the "Singles Party," I visit the Grand Salon. Groups have formed, couples begin to link with other couples; the various age brackets are drawn to one another. "I whisked him away," a wife says to another about her husband. "He works too hard. How about yours?" The other wife thinks for a moment. "I talked him into the cruise," she admits. "Wanted him to go before he has a heart attack." The men were not in sight.

The singles cocktail party is in session. The social

hostess takes her problems with professional aplomb. I can see her dilemma: I count twenty ladies, some of whom are in their seventies, and only four men. The two best-looking girls have already decided on their escorts for the voyage. The rest of the passengers remind me of the Ark of Noah; they all arrived in twos. For most of them, every night will be New Year's Eve, with dancing and night-clubbing long after midnight. A Mexican fiesta, a costume-masquerade evening, a Las Vegas night with roulette and other gambling, Bingo, chuck-a-luck and horse racing, a discotheque contest, many parties, apart from movies, bridge contests, and various lectures. Fortunately, no one pressures us to participate.

Because we land in Puerto Vallarta tomorrow, I listen to an orientation talk. It includes lessons on how to bargain. "Pay only one-third of what they ask," I'm told. "And don't panic if the merchants speak Spanish." Good advice.

Tuesday

Puerto Vallarta! Some of the three hundred passengers split into groups that descended upon the curio shops. Others go on a sightseeing tour. I opt for a boat trip to Yelapa, a small remote cove. This side trip has been billed as "adventurous"; the elderly get a warning that they may not be comfortable. We step on a launch that takes us onto a heaving excursion boat, the *El Sombrero*. For two hours, all the way to Yelapa, we bounce and trounce, pitch from side to side. To reach our final destination, we're transferred into dugout canoes. Six "adventurers" can go at a time, and I volunteer. The canoes' benches remind me of swings that fly up and down, down and up. But I manage to sit down, shoes in my lap. The native oarsmen make speed, and slice the high waves in five minutes. We jump off onto the sandy crescent of Yelapa beach. Most of us are wet but happy. I watch the next canoe come in like a landing barge. The waves shoot up as high as the thatched restaurant huts. Imprisoned in the canoes, our lady tourists give one long scream. Some fifty shipmates join us this way, a mighty American invasion force, with mighty good lungs. Where are the movie people when we need them? And so on, day by day, until the final farewell on the last day.

We land at 8:00 A.M. The Grand Salon is choking with passengers, saying their farewells, often several times. "Well, good-bye. Good-bye again." We line up at passport control. Some of the people look a bit distant now, again like strangers. The slings and arrows of real life are closing in. One of the older men tells one of the widows at our table, "I'll visit you in Joliet." But he sounds half-hearted, and I doubt if she believes him.

As the people go down the gangplank, some of the crew members wave lightly, perhaps already thinking about the next passengers that come aboard in a few hours. One couple actually stays on the ship; they're doing it again.

My own cruise has come to an end. The queue at immigration control moves forward. Somehow I feel a pang of nostalgia at leaving this ship. I can see the smog outside, and I know that it will be cold at home. The official opens my passport.

"Welcome back," he says.

Writer's Block

"For the moment I have lost faith in my capacity to write. I feel written out," confesses one well-known author to her journal. It is a recurring theme; you find it in many journals of famous authors. For the professional who must write to pay for groceries and rent, no affliction is worse. The reasons for a sudden stoppage vary. Psychiatrist Dr. Theodore Rubin once gave a long, enlightening lecture to the American Society of Journalists and Authors on the topic. Here are some of the points Dr. Rubin made:

Each problem of writer's block is unique to the individual, and each represents a different set of psychodynamics. The variations in the problems that prevail are great. In some cases writers suffer depression. In others there is intense anxiety. In some there is a combination of both. If a writer's personal life is bad, if he or she is going through a difficult situation, he or she might experience a block. The block is a symbol of the disturbed psychological state. Writer's block can erupt when the writer has strained relationships with a publisher, an agent, or an editor. Some writers experience a block the moment they receive a signed contract. Others block *until* they receive the contract. One of the biggest blocks is perfectionism—when a writer believes, for example, that he or she is doing highly important work and refuses to settle for less.

Just what are the remedies for the blockage? One psychologist offers some good advice, perfect for *this* book. She advises that you hurry to your diary. "The writer's log is the biggest tool for an author who can't produce," says Dr. Karin Mack, who is rated as a leading U.S. expert on the subject. She adds: "Write down *why* you can't write!"

Presumably, this gets you to writing again, and the momentum will keep you at it. One well-known New England author used this Rx with great success; she sorted out on paper some of the reasons for her (now past) difficulties.

My own remedy, like that of some other professionals, is to turn to a favorite book. Let another author inspire you, making you want to compete a little. You might call it priming the pump.

Good health habits, exercise, getting away from the typewriter on occasion, choosing the best hour for your writing chores are all helpful, too. Dr. Rubin suggests that you reduce your expectations of yourself and that you try to find people who support your writing. Dr. Rubin's final advice: "If all fails, try free-associating on paper. Simply write down notes and comments about your subject, without regard as to whether they are good or bad, well-written or not, poorly organized or not. After you collect a page or two of these notes, you might feel more encouraged, and it will begin to generate better morale."

We return full circle to Dr. Sidney Werkman, who encouraged new diary-writers to try this technique.

6

A Sample Diary

Selections from the Author's Journals

February 10, 1943

Dear Diary: Have you ever had a toothache? No, you haven't because you're just a diary! Be glad! I'm suffering for three days now. Lot's of pills. None effective. Maybe I should have it pulled. But there is no dentist right now. My army buddies say I shouldn't think about the toothache. They have it easy; their teeth don't hurt! I can't sleep!

February 12, 1943

The dentist made it into this camp. The tooth is out!

June 2, 1959

I now have children of my own! They're now 5½ and 4½ and full of questions. What's that up there? A horseshoe. For horses? Yes. But you don't have any horses. Why is it up there? For luck. Luck? What's that? That's a good question. We don't have any luck, baby. What's luck? Oh, lots of money and lots of health and happy children and—

Carla loves paper. She collects it, in all colors. Then she cuts it with scissors, and very deftly, too, stuffs it into her miniature handbag. And how she loves to paint! Her drawings make sense these days. There is the bright sun, yellow, bordered by red or mauve; there are the clouds, which look like balls of wool; there are the houses with rectangular windows and the door at the right spot. Flowers grow about the house, and she has colored the flowers. A hare sits in the grass.

Stevie likes water colors, and when he paints with them all is wet: the table, the floor, his clothes.

He also likes to irritate his sister; the more she screams, the merrier. He cuddles up in Daddy's lap, puts his satiny hands on Daddy's face.

They can ski, too, although they still don't know how to lean forward. Later, if they fall, one must help them up; they yell as though their legs are broken. And in the end they are so tired that we must carry their skis back.

July 2, 1966

I'm in Flachau, Austria. In front of my window, beyond the flower boxes with geraniums, I can see a thick, green vale of meadow unrolling to ascend toward more chalets. I see a pink church with a red onion-shaped steeple. The daisies stand knee high, and hazelnut bushes flank a gurgling stream.

Somehow, Europe's relentless line of honking and fuming autos still hasn't penetrated this valley about fifty-five miles south of Salzburg. It's peaceful enough, yet there are horses for riding, paths for hiking, two outdoor swimming pools, an occasional band at night, a wine *stueberl,* and restaurants serving veal cutlets at a dollar a head.

My room is one of several in a farm home. It's comfortable, with thick, old Austrian furniture. A breakfast of fresh rolls, coffee, and egg is included in the price.

January 2, 1968

Dental problems!

Dr. B. is a big man, totally bald, with violent jowls and heavy hands. He might be a butcher and emerge from one of those ads, "Learn Meatcutting!" He's astonishingly clumsy and rough; he tests the solidity of my teeth with large, sausage-shaped fingers, almost pulls one out that way. He points with his sharp instruments, stabs the x-ray panel, where my choppers are hung up like so many skeletons, then at once jabs the sharp tool back into my mouth. His voice is booming as he shows me the dentures he's made, with crowns. He speaks for almost an hour, then concludes: "I'm not a salesman. I'm a doctor, I want to heal," in a voice that still rings in my ears. When I tell him others want to extract every tooth, he counters, "They're *meschugge.*" When I tell him that the infection in my gums might be dangerous, he says, "You look healthy. You eat good. So you have a little *Schmutz* in gums. Lots of people have. . . ."

January 3, 1968

Dr. W. surrounds himself with sexy nurses; their grins are much too bright; their dresses much too tight. You can see that they've been trained to reassure the patient, but the idea of extractions makes me feel like an old man. W. asks no questions, insists upon taking x-rays. "Look at B.'s," he says. "They're much too faded." But when W.'s own x-rays are finished they just as faded and gray, and two teeth have been only half photographed. W. arrives with a metal tray—not unlike those that hung in the showers of cheap motels, for the soap—shoves it unceremoniously (and without explanation) over my upper teeth. "I'm only measuring." Then he returns with another filled tray: it contains some sort of evil-tasting paste. He shoves it into my mouth. "I must take an impression." When he wants to do the same to lowers, I protest, for the center tooth is totally loose and would adhere to the paste. But W. insists: "We won't let you go without teeth; we'll put a new one in, I assure you." I say no. And down comes the chair. I escape!

January 24, 1968

Dr. C. is the calmest of the lot, the most dignified, with sharp lines in his large face. He's said to be a society dentist . . . Coors, Boettchers . . . and to be an expert at dentures. Indeed, his x-ray technician (he, too, must take his own, but he assures me, "There's no charge for these") has some interesting gimmicks; a toothbrush type of stick moves into the mouth, presses the x-ray tabs against the teeth. . . . She's so fast that she almost knocks out one tooth, my loose one. (Outside the leaves are falling.) Dr. C. surrounded by some six smiling assistants (young girls who flurry hither and thither), comes up with the grim verdict that it'll cost at least $2,000. I ask him to take out the totally loose tooth, and to my astonishment, he comes with a piece of string. "It's the old-fashioned method, you know . . . remember how it was as a child?" But the tooth doesn't come out, and he has to use the forceps nevertheless, which he does fast and deftly. . . .

January 2, 1970

I read Johann Wolfgang von Goethe. An English translation. He writes: "Ingratitude is always a form of weakness. I have never known a person of real ability to be ungrateful . . ."

So true!

May 18, 1975

A new class at the local Free University. "How to Meet People without Going to a Bar." I never go to bars, anyway, but I'd like to know how people get along these days. What bugs them? What expectations to they have? The man in charge believes in yoga, deep breathing. Esalen-type touch-thy-neighbor-and-feel-less-alone groping, touching in the dark. Circles formed, arms around strangers.

The encounter workshop is run by a mysterious young man (he doesn't want to speak about his background or degrees). He says he aims for a "group feeling": a circle is formed as though for an Israeli or a Greek dance. Deep breathing *together*. The second session—this time in Cheeseman Park—pursues the same direction but in a most juvenile and kindergarten way: We are to hold hands and race through the park, single file, like tiny tots! More Esalen: the lifting of one body by four or five people. The person is held aloft for a few minutes. I don't like to participate in such group-oriented games. Ideas seem more important. We have a brief respite from the childish games. We finally sit down to talk. A young woman complains (justly, I think) about the lack of honesty among her peers. The group at once chided her for such negative thoughts. Indeed, *no* one of the forty or fifty people backed her! Until I got on a soapbox and scolded the entire class. The leader said nothing.

May 29, 1975

A few seconds that could have changed everything—life to death or life to crippling injury. It is 12:05 P.M. I'm at the Western National Bank to get some cash. I wait while the teller looks into her ledgers. Someone grabs me from behind. But not hard enough to [make me] suspect more than a prank.

I turn and see a hideous mask—Halloween style, plus yellow gloves, plus a sawed-off shotgun. Someone in the bank shouts "Down!" And down go the tellers and secretaries and a few customers. (Will the bandit stay or shoot?)

I fall to the ground myself, and . . . a shot rings out. I start crawling rapidly for cover, as they taught us in the World War II army. My breath comes fast. Another shot! I see a bank officer getting to his feet. The first faces emerge above the back counters. I get up and notice the bandit collapsed on the floor. (It turns out that the guard had shot him as soon as I'd crawled away.) The robber is still alive, although I later learned that he was shot through the lungs. A second stickup man, standing at the door, had pulled his trigger, in the direction of the guard. But the bandit's bullet didn't fly. Instead, the guard shot him, too.

A third man was held outside at gunpoint by an ex-Marine. My own thoughts flipped from "It can't be real" to "Oh, no, not that!" to "Will I die?"

It later appears that I was to be the hostage. But I totally startled and confused the thugs by crawling away, and thus may have foiled their whole plot. The feat still pulsates through me, making my chest rise high with every heartbeat.

Within minutes afterward, the bank was full of cops and detectives and back personnel (one of whom amused me by saying, "Sorry to have inconvenienced you!").

The greater inconvience followed: A trip to the seedy, rundown, claustrophobic, downtown police department, long waits, long interrogations (as though *we* committed the crime!), swearing that we spoke the truth, FBI interviews, waiting for a car back to the bank. Not a good experience for a slight paranoic like myself. When I complained, a beefy-faced detective told me: "You're lucky to be alive."

So I was.

June 19, 1975

A seven-day trip to Utah. E. is as adaptable, practical, handy as always. She pumps gas at self-service stations to save us a few pennies; she directs a flat-tire operation so capably that we do the job in ten minutes, quickly enough to come punctually to a dinner invitation. E. helps drive, gathers wood, fills the mountain air with her enthusiasm about the scenery. Makes love eagerly every night, shows enough poise and savvy at the workshop. She mixes well, acquires friends easily, gets along with all the ladies.

Niwot Ridge, Colorado *September 1, 1976*

Encircling clouds that blot out the valley within minutes. The mountains disappear and we feel the first rain. The zigzag of lightning across the crests.

We're off trail and looking for an escape. The rain pours as we find our steep path. While we walk, the rain turns it into a small brook and we can feel our boots beginning to squish. Within half an hour, we're wet to the skin—we haven't taken parkas—and the flashes come closer, directly overhead now. We descend at a more rapid pace, through deeper and deeper waters.

The adventure tastes good on our lips. It takes at least ninety minutes to reach our campground. Relief: we open E.'s van door. The mattress, sheets, towels beckon. The world around us seems to crash and dissolve, with sheets of water running down the glass panes.

But, we're warm. For our return home, we decide not to take the E.P. route, but use the peak-to-peak highway instead.

Just then, the radio tells about the flood in the Thompson Canyon.

It cost two hundred lives. But oh God in heaven, not ours.

September 30, 1976

It's hard to believe. We still talked about death on our last evening, just two weeks ago. E. said she never thought of death because "there was so much living to do." So true.

She lived life to the hilt. She took it all in, the hikes, adventures, music, people (how she loved people!), Pyrenees dogs, travel, films, photography. One last picture—one last shot, her friend Carol said, her face pale, when I told her about E.'s tragic fall. She had no fear of heights, of course, and she was not a suicidal person. But that Delphi scene—that lone little acropolis up there—must have made her forget the rules of gravity for just one instant. The picture! The picture no doubt counted in the moment more than life itself.

My son N., during one of our walks, talked about

E., whom he liked. He said she would have been good insurance for my old age. Her traces are all over my house. And will be hard to erase.

I considered a psychiatrist today. Instead I'll read *Someone You Love Is Dying*. It should be "E. M. Has Died."

And much too suddenly.

October 1, 1976

E. is to be buried at the little cemetery in Rhodes; the thought makes me melancholy. Almost every waking moment somehow leads to the memory of her—just now I showed someone my garden, and there were E.'s roses, her tomatoes, raspberries, the stakes she'd set, the table she had brought. I've cried a little. I could cry all the time. I feel inconsolable. My entire life has been turned around.

Corky S., a psychologist and friend, tells me that I must date soon, that I must keep busy to lessen the pain. My son, Stephen, came to a rescue, with lunch and beer and a long walk. But I know that I must do it myself, work through the grief.

October 3, 1976

Countermeasures: long hikes, running, tennis, conversations with R., talks with Stephen.

E. will be hard to replace. Not only because of her warmth, decency, femininity, generosity, artistry, but also because she was so practical. She could fix anything. My car tires and even plumbing. She planted the garden and cut my hair and gave my parties, sowed, sewed, and salved physical wounds. Hail, E., out there under the blue Greek sky. There won't be another one like you!

Is grief self-pity? So many people say so because E. is *well* now—feeling no pain. Can grieving be stopped? Not now, surely. Not now just when I feel this great loss, when I realize that I must start from the beginning—when the best person has been wrenched from my side. "She wouldn't want you to sorrow so much," say the psychologists. "He who deliberately retains overindulgence in grief willfully makes himself miserable," writes one psychiatrist. "Overwhelming grief is a concession to fear—your loss has left you lonely—prey to the reminder that you, too, are vulnerable to death . . . ." This is so true although my piqued fear is that of the immediate future—to get along *without* her wonderful company. "Develop mastery over yourself," counsels this psychiatrist. Ah! *Qui vivra verra* is one consolation. Who lives shall see.

November 12, 1976

The scene at one unnamed singles meeting holds no charms for me. The dance seems superimportant to these people. The music is loud, jarring. I'm not ready for it. Too soon. At 10:00 P.M. someone suggests a "rap session" at a private home in a faraway suburb. It proved to be a pointless exercise in listening to a rap leader who held the floor 80 percent of the time. The man was superficial. He kept switching from an account of his (silly) dates to flood victims to "rapport between people." I had no rapport with him at all. Most of the talk was abstract. When I spoke about the pain and trauma of losing E., the assembled singles seemed astonished and quickly changed the subject.

November 13, 1976

Strange dream last night. I was sailing on a cruise ship and there, in my cabin, I suddenly saw E.!

Saw her as clearly as if she were alive. Hugged her. And felt the deepest joy . . . as well as a little embarrassment . . . what to do about all those obituaries? That published magazine article tracing her life?

Felt all the past love, all the affection. Visualized a fresh life for us ahead. Then, alas, I came awake, and knew that it had only been a fantasy. The result: I couldn't sleep the rest of the night. Even after so many weeks, she is still there with me.

February 20, 1977

Two days with son Niccolo, who is very mature now. Doesn't have to be the first one on the ski lift, or the last one to leave the slopes, like five years ago. And he knows that he skis superbly, so he doesn't have to prove anything to his father. No more downhill runs that scare the daylights out of me, but runs that seem perfect for this aging sportsman.

And although he has problems to solve—mostly about girls—he remains in good balance, sensitive, open to new ideas, versatile, interested in so many things; in sum, a delight.

The ski areas themselves, by contrast, are madhouses. Oh, 16,000 skiers at Vail! Trampling one another on and off the slope. How ironic! Here's an activity that was supposed to take us away from people, *from* the city—

Aspen, Colorado *June 6, 1977*

How strange to return to a place thirty years later! I arrived here almost thirty years ago, alone. I came back again, alone. Yet how much happened in the interim! Eighteen years of marriage to a smart, cold woman. Three children, who are scattered across the globe. Relationships, some of them beautiful; some of them senseless. An obstacle-filled, finally soaring career. Travel to the four corners.

I went to a cheery tennis class and then drove up to the Maroon Bells campground and ate alone, face to face with the noble Maroon Bells. How symmetric they are! How perfect the curve of the valley and the embedded crater lake! Divine mountains and glorious solitude! My fried Vienna sausages and tomatoes tasted like a gourmet meal. It is good that on occasion I like my own company.

September 15, 1977

E.'s death anniversary will soon be here. But I'm girded for combat. New classes en masse. Work aplenty.

September 24, 1977

What a lovely day! After a good breakfast, Niccolo and I repair to the sun-flooded tennis courts. The scene is all ours. No one else at the park! I'm grateful that I can still run after the ball, at my age. Grateful for the thirst afterward. Our hunger is stilled by a crunchy loaf of black bread, fresh Bibb salad, boiled shrimp with a mustard dressing, gallons of iced tea! In the afternoon, I drive to the mountains with M.G., to hike. Ah, there is always the light at the end of the tunnel!

May 18, 1978

Son Stephen is back for a few weeks.

He looks physically changed—no longer the pimply boy but a man, clear of skin, erect, beard carefully trimmed, eyes leveling with you. He's handsome in a Lawrence of Arabia fashion—all ruggedness, with his broad shoulders, light-blue eyes. (They used to be darker and were quite direct.)

I'm proud of him and love him, with his physical change—and his sojourn in Morocco—there obviously came an inner change, of course.

He's deeper, more silent, slightly less responsive to the world around him, more withdrawn.

He's more one-dimensional, too, made so by his great love, pride, possession—his Moslem religion. It is his be-all and end-all; even Stephen's future wife seems to be an instrument, a vessel not of love but of deepening the commitment to Allah. Extraordinary!

I love him no less for it. I think that there could be a worse route—crime, for instance. More, I must (& do) accept Stephen's conversion and his slowly growing away from our values (for which he has contempt, I think). He's himself, an adult who decides the course of his own life.

May 28, 1978

Refreshing day at the Broadmoor Resort with son Niccolo. Fleeting pleasures, but pleasures all the same: A trout *au bleu* for me, steak Diane for him. Tennis in the morning, amid the green, green lawns, the well-kept shrubbery, the beds of petunias. Eggs Benedict for breakfast at the golf-course restaurant. Niccolo is adaptable, and intelligent, mature, always interesting. But the boy in him still comes out for a moment when he wants to drive an electric golf cart.

June 13, 1978

Another singles "rap" session. Topic: "How do we feel about ourselves?" I suggest that our self-esteem would increase if we were more human beings, less *plastic*. If we had more sympathy, more empathy, listened more to others, gave love and accepted love.

The group leader called me an idealist.

A woman insisted that we must "package" ourselves; we'd feel better if we dressed better. The group's conversation then switched to clothes altogether. No allies here for more depth, alas!

July 7, 1978

The tragedy of modern American life seems to be the scarcity of friendship. How rare intimacy has become! And how we rejoice when we finally have it! Is [it] the transient society or the sexual revolution that creates so much superficiality? And that defeats all chances for close relationships? We meet someone and ask important questions. But we receive no answers; the person is afraid of someone getting too close. We date an individual who may be intelligent and has mate-companion potential, only to learn that we face a wall, a closed door. Some Americans retreat quickly behind a polite facade; it is difficult to come forward, to reach out.

August 20, 1978

Was stimulated by a magazine article entitled "Obsessed with Love." How true! "There's only one thing that causes misery—unfulfilled expectations!" Ah, yes, how we yearn, how we hope to find just a little more love . . . and indeed, our expectations, even reasonable ones, remain so often unfulfilled. "Never ask for more than a woman can give," a psychologist once told me. I accepted his advice with my head, but alas, when it comes to the heart, my dear, even Marcia Seligson's wise words are no more than words . . . an impossibility to achieve.

We are human; we *do* have expectations, and if they're not met, we go away disappointed even if we tell ourselves, intellectually, that we must not ask for so much. Isn't that so? And don't we all suffer because we hope for a certain measure of affection and so seldom get it?

There is a certain woman I took to the mountains over a weekend recently. Harmonious trip, civilized conversation, good vibes, brief meeting of the minds. But when I got back from the West Coast and phoned, she was curt. She had visitors at home. She promised to call me when she had time, but she never did. I had hoped—yearned!—for continued affection, a genuine relationship, warmth, even on the phone. Instead, there was coldness; maybe it had just been a brief adventure to her. One morning she called, full of tears. I drove to the apartment; she'd had some family problem; when I tried to console her, soothe her, she chided me for my mean male logic, claiming that only she had the emotions! Ah, we're indeed like the ships that pass in the night, the faces only fleeting shadows. "Life's but a walking shadow, a poor player / That struts and frets his hour upon the stage / And then is heard no more," as Shakespeare wrote, meaning that an ultimate emptiness, death itself, awaits us all.

March 2, 1979

The Loom

Dear Weaver,

I like your multihued threads that add up to a tapestry of many parts: the Alpine snow wet, almost too bright, as our skis claw their way upward. The sea gulls diving into Sloan's Lake for last week's brioches, while at elevation ten thousand the hungry jays ignore our carrots. The rain's signature, all circles, on Gem Lake. Beaver's Village disappears behind us: a blizzard white as the goose down that clothes us. The strands multiply: season's first crocus, ancient lichen on rock, four bare feet racing through the Pacific salt spray, a country store (oval mirrors adorned with owls), nocturnal visits, blood singing in our veins. Two bodies become one, intertwine like the strongest fabric. Amicable talk at dawn when we should sleep. A Mazatlán breakfast: red, green, orange melon. Lime wedges. On the beach, mariachis, vendors of kites and crucifixes. Then, the coffee-colored woman with a Madonna smile. A cargo of carpets.

Ah, si! She made them herself. I look at you.
Admit it, Helen. You've been weaving, too,
with your age-old loom
of love.

Keystone Lodge, Colorado *July 6, 1979*

My father always said that one must be a *Lebenskünstler*. I think he was right—and I pursue the art of living as he did. In these mountains, one can arrange both one's meals and times for maximum enjoyment. Breakfast outdoors by the Swiss-looking lake, for instance, with the eggs beaming under the sun. The glass table surrounded by cunningly placed beds of daisies. No restaurant at dusk; instead, the lakeside (Dillon Lake) picnic. Preparations at 7:00 P.M., when the sun gives off one final blast before it disappears behind the peaks. A slowly cooking *ratatouille* of fresh and canned vegetables, cool bottles of beer. When the clouds still glow a little overhead, some fresh fruit and a brandy in bed— *a deux*, of course. (We start making love in the middle of the news—a much more comforting action than the newscaster's litany of disasters.) Then sleep, sleep and the knowledge of another Alpine hike. *"Lebenskünst!"*

August 29, 1979

A chronicle of . . . Trips to faraway places; in this case, North Africa. Thus: I visit Stephen's land in the Oreka Valley via Marrakesh, Morocco. Mountains flow behind his olive trees. We water Stephen's young peaches. We walk. We help the hired man encourage a donkey that doesn't want to work.

We eat fruit under grape arbors. Save for the sounds of animals—a few dogs and chickens and toads—the country is very quiet. At night you see the stars.

Very refreshing and contrasting with Marrakesh—a city that seems too tense and angry and bustling.

Naturally, Stephen and Fatima's modern prayers—five times a day—make sense out there in the country. They want to build their house on this land . . . in a year or two. And then have children.

January 7, 1980

Cross-country skiing Copper Mountain under brightest sky. It had snowed the night before; the fir trees powdered by that great pastry chef in the sky. Brooks frozen and snow-covered. But I can hear the whispering sounds of the water under the ice. I emerge from the shade; the brook water is suddenly visible, flowing over stones, a transparent moving film, cool and swishing. Around the ice edges, smaller, sharper scallops of thinner ice, which is in turn covered by perfect little half doilies of snow. I walk steadily on my skis. Stop to look. Slide again with joy among the snow mounds, under the trees. How clean it all is! What a contrast to the filthy cities! How we *need nature!*

February 13, 1980

I avoid chronically angry women. Not long after my divorce, I briefly went with a San Francisco feminist whose every second word was "chauvinist!" The mere mention of a possible Sierra hike, or a certain trail—made her rebel against me. "You're trying to dictate! Chauvinist!" I was only suggesting. Deeply troubled then, she is still not a happy person today.

Nor am I certain whether an abrasive Betty Friedan can bring happiness to either women or men. There must have been five of us writers standing in a circle one New York evening. Suddenly Betty Friedan, a member of our organization, burst through the door. She bore down on our group in her leather jacket.

The author of *The Feminine Mystique* next elbowed her way into the circle of men. (I'm not saying that she started the idea of "battered men" in America, but she certainly gave us pause to think.)

As a male, I also consider Bella Abzug types too extreme. Their belligerence often works against them. Their macholike line docs little for their (just) causes. ("Men are frightened of tough women," says a psychologist. "Intimidation isn't a good thing for either sex.") By contrast, Gloria Steinem always gave me good vibes. She is assertive yet still a woman who never lost her charm or femininity. "I don't intend to wear combat boots or cut off my hair," she once explained. Bravo, more power to her.

I admire women who go about their business quietly and effectively. I could easily vote for a woman as president.

Many experts feel that the leather-jacketed Friedan is passé. Out of style. Anthropologist Susan Byrne, a friend, predicts that women will again become more feminine. And while the male's original gender role has given way to the sensitive, emoting, caring Liberated Man, some of his strength and aggressiveness will return.

To my mind, when all is said and done between the sexes, only one thing matters. The ability to give and receive affection. Ultimately, in psychiatrist Viktor Frankl's words, "Our salvation is only through and in love—"

February 12, 1980

A woman friend is coming to dinner.

I shopped earlier this afternoon. Delicate lamb chops, a Bibb salad, Camembert cheese, a fresh pineapple. I polish the wine glasses, set the table, adorn it with candles, fresh flowers in a vase. While the chops are braising, I clean, slice, brandy our tropical fruit. My friend arrives at 9:00 P.M. Everything is ready. I serve, of course, and don't expect her to wash the dishes. We make love instead.

The Liberated Male? I believe that a woman is entitled to the same salary as a man. I'm for the ERA. I applaud women's achievements in the arts, the sciences, politics. And all of my male friends accept the newly minted female engineers, crane operators, truck drivers. There are many, many women lawyers. And about one-third of this country's psychiatric interns are women. And why not? We now live in an age of equality and free choices.

April 30, 1980

Back from ten productive days in Mexico. James Pinto, the international painter, finally opened my eyes to contemporary art. He paints ideas, his inner life, visions and not figures or objects. He paints what he wants. He doesn't compromise.

Mexico itself is a tiring land, despite its quiet corners; the country demands that we accept a totally different mode of life. Driving through D.F.—fortunately with our Mexican guide at the wheel of his souped-up '72 Mercury—was a roller-coaster ride. What speeds! What near-misses in traffic accidents! Even our Mexicana di Aviacion pilot banked a little harder and hit the landing gear with more passion than average pilots. The food was an almost constant catastrophe . . . fat, uncooked meats; beef like shoe leather; trout no larger than Maine sardines; soups so bland that we begin to doubt Mexico's traditional spicing. The slowest of service, the most monstrous city traffic.

But also the beauty: dark-eyed children; women who hark back to the Aztec and Mayan portraits by Diego Rivera; lovingly dressed babies of less than a year; and the soft nights on the plaza when all of San Miguel de Allende seems to walk by, passing the Spanish churches, under the eternal Mexican stars.

May 10, 1980

"Go up into the mountains. Your body needs it. And your soul, too," read the sign in Austria. We went up into the Rockies today. And it's all true, as always. Only natural things can give such joys. The clouds sailing overhead, the rain-scrubbed faces of those glacier slopes, the wind-polished fir trees.

Small inconvenience: The snow.

We trooped upward through it until our boots were soaked, soaked. My heels actually started smarting.

We lunched on a rocky ledge. Cheese, bread, and tea—a feast, under the circumstances.

And I feel pleasantly tired now and at peace with the world.

June 10, 1980

Our heavy winter has been followed by the briefest of springs and a spectacular summer. Ah, what an abundance of mountain flowers! On a hike this morning, I could spot all kinds of unfamiliar flora in the foothills. The sun shone.

All was well with this writer's world . . . even the birds sang in unison.

July 26, 1980

Pleasant Saturday morning stroll around Sloan's Lake. During the 4½ miles, we saw:

- A large Korean family fishing for carp. Even the smallest children had long homemade poles.
- Four American families with gleaming motorboats pulling water skiers. The average age was twenty to twenty-five. What an affluent society!
- A couple lulling under an enormous tent. Both reclining in chairs.
- Bicyclists and runners with long moustaches, and a jogger who probably weighed three hundred pounds.
- An enormously fat lady in shorts with a fat dog.
- An old man watching his five fishing rods from the inside of a big, old-fashioned car.
- A gaggle of Canadian geese flying, single file, over the motor boats.

November 12, 1980

My love affair with ocean cruises continues, especially this time. The voyage is all insouciance: I have unfurled my papers and uncovered the typewriter; it is set up on a table as long as I could wish, in a cabin as spacious as my Lowell Blvd. office. Outside the porthole, the blue carpet of the calm ocean unrolls alongside the vessel; the white seams of sunny waves race across the high ceiling of my stateroom. The steward has brought iced tea; I'm settling down to another ten pages of the book, I'm whittling away at the task until it is done.

Earlier this morning, the obligatory table tennis tournament. I lost against a Swiss passenger 22-20. Near me, people were in the pool, which made its own waves, copying the sea around us. On four levels, hundreds of mostly ancient bodies on deck chairs. Not quietly, of course; most of the folks here chatter all the time. And the *Veendam is* another Ark of Noah: all couples of various sizes and appetites.

A little later, I go to lunch on the Lido deck. The Dutch treat us well: masses of fruit from Europe, the United States, the tropics. Holland's famous cheeses. Hot dishes. Pastries. Urns of coffee, with taps indicating its strength. (Very considerate, that.)

November 21, 1980

Outdoor experiences:

If we really return to this earth as animals, let it be an Eskimo dog for me!

I walked for 1½ hours to the post office through a snowstorm just now. Enjoyed every moment of it—even the flakes biting my face, the chill penetrating my wool cap.

I grinned all the way to my destination. A long walk, punctuated by the spinning of many wheels. Cars swerved and struggled. But I found myself on foot, leaping across the Arctic snows . . . .

7

The Diary in Religion, Literature, and History

In order to improve one's diary skills, nothing would seem more valuable than studying the journals of others. Through the ages diaries have taken many forms, from the formalized, day-by-day account of a historical figure to the autobiographical notes that range back and forth through a lifetime.

One typical example, that of St. Augustine, covers the years from A.D. 354 to A.D. 387. Seldom has a writer expressed a greater religious fervor or summoned so much eloquence as St. Augustine, philosopher, theologian, and priest. What emotion he brings to his faith!

The following excerpts are from St. Augustine, *Confessions,* translated by R. S. Pine-Coffin, Penguin Classics, King's Road, London, England, 1961. Reprinted by permission.

A.D. 354 to A.D. 387: Saint Augustine: *Confessions*

Can any praise be worthy of the Lord's majesty? How magnificent his strength! How inscrutable his wisdom! Man is one of your creatures, Lord, and his instinct is to praise you. He bears about him the mark of death, the sign of his own sin, to remind him that you *thwart the proud.* But still, since he is a part of your creation, he wishes to praise you. The thought of you stirs him so deeply that he cannot be content unless he praises you, because you made us for yourself and our hearts find no peace until they rest in you.

Grant me, Lord, to know and understand whether a man is first to pray to you for help or to praise you, and whether he must know you before he can call you to his aid. If he does not know you, how can he pray to you? For he may call for some other help, mistaking it for yours.

Or are men to pray to you and learn to know you through their prayers? *Only, how are they to call upon the Lord until they have learned to believe in him? And how are they to believe in him without a preacher to listen to?*

* * *

I asked him why it was then that the future was often correctly foretold by means of astrology. He gave me the only possible answer, that it was all due to the power of chance, a force that must always be reckoned with in the natural order. He said that people sometimes opened a book of poetry at random, and although the poet had been thinking, as he wrote, of some quite different matter, it often happened that the reader placed his finger on a verse that had a remarkable bearing on his problem. It was not surprising, then, that the mind of man, quite unconsciously, through some instinct not within its own control, should hit upon some thing that answered to the circumstances and the facts of a particular question. If so, it would be due to chance not to skill.

This answer that he gave me, or rather that I heard from his lips, must surely have come from you, my God. By means of it you imprinted on my mind doubts that I was to remember later, when I came to argue these matters out for myself. But at that time neither he nor my great friend, Nebridius—a young man of high principles and unexceptionable character, who ridiculed the whole business of soothsaying—could persuade me to give it up. I thought that the authors of the books made out a better case, and I had as yet found no evidence as positive as I required to prove beyond doubt that when the astrologers were found to be right, it was due to luck or pure chance and not to their skill in reading the stars.

* * *

Crimes against other men are committed when the emotions, which spur us to action, are corrupt and rise in revolt without control. Sins of self-indulgence are committed when the soul fails to govern the impulses from which it derives bodily pleasure. In the same way, if the rational mind is corrupt, mistaken ideas and false beliefs will poison life. In those days my mind was corrupt. I did not know that if it was to share in the truth, it must be illumined by another light because the mind itself is not the essence of truth. For *it is you, Lord, that keep the lamp of my hopes still burning and shine on the darkness about me.*

* * *

How wonderful are your Scriptures! How profound! We see their surface and it attracts us like children. And yet, O my God, their depth is stupendous. We shudder to peer deep into them, for they inspire in us both the awe of reverence and the thrill of love.

Thanks be to you, O Lord, for all that we see!

We see heaven and earth, which may be either the upper and the lower parts of the material world or the spiritual and material creations. For their adornment, whether they continue the whole of the material world or the entire creation, spiritual and material alike, we see the light that was created and separated from the darkness. We see the firmament of heaven, by which we may understand either the uppermost part of the material world, which divides the spiritual waters above from the material waters below, or simply the space of air through which the birds take flight. For this space also is called the heavens, and it divides the waters that rise in the form of vapor and descend again on calm nights, distilled in the form of dew, from those that are heavier and flow upon the earth. We see the waters gathered together, so that the surface of the sea is like a great plain, and the dry land, first rising bare from the waters and then with form added so that it might become visible and order might be given to it and it should become the mother of plants and trees. We see the lights shining from above, the sun furnishing its light to the day and the moon and the stars giving comfort to the night, and all of them marking the passage of time.

* * *

Accept my confessions, O Lord. They are a sacrifice offered by my tongue, for yours was the hand that fashioned it and yours the spirit that moved it to acknowledge you. Heal all my bones and let them say *Lord, there is none like you.*

1748-1776: George Washington: *Day by Day*

Let's take a big leap across the Middle Ages to early America, where the first U.S. President, George Washington (who was born in 1732 and died in 1799), knew his debt to history: He catalogued his daily duties, along with some reflections. The brevity of the notes stands out today. The *Day by Day* material was published in New York in 1895, and the occasional introduction to the diary entries was written by Elisabeth Bryant Johnson, one of George Washington's early biographers.

March 13, 1748

"Rode to his Lordship's Quarters, (Greenway Court, seat of Lord Fairfax) about four miles up ye river. Went through most beautiful groves of maple, spent ye best of ye day admiring ye Trees and ye richness of ye land."

April 2, 1748

George Washington when surveying in the Shenandoah Valley noted in his journal: "Last night was a blowing rainy night. Our straw catch'd a Fire, we were laying upon. We did two Lots & was attended by a great Company of People, men, women, & children, that attended us through ye woods as we went, shewing their antick tricks. I really think they seem to be as ignorant a set of people as the Indians. They would never speak English but when spoken to, they speak all Dutch."

December 31, 1753

"I went up about three miles to the Mouth of Youghiogany to visit Queen Aliquippa, who had expressed great concern that we passed her in going to the Fort. I made her a Present of a Watchcoat and a Bottle of Rum; which latter was thought much the better Present of the Two."

January 28, 1760

Washington, always busy, never overlooked laziness in others. He wrote in his diary: "Visited my plantation, severely reprimanded young Stephens for indolence, and his father for suffering it. Found the new Negro, Cupid, ill with pleurisy at Dogue Run, and had him brought home in a cart for better care of him."

February 12, 1768

"Went fox-hunting with Colonel Fairfax, Mr. McCarty, Mr. Chichester, Captains Posey and Manley, who dined here with Mrs. Fairfax and Miss Nichols. Catched two foxes."

January 15, 1776

The commander-in-chief, discouraged by delays and sectional strife. "I have often thought how much happier I should have been, if, instead of accepting the command under such circumstances, I had taken my musket on my shoulder and entered the ranks, or if I could have justified the measure to posterity, and my own conscience, had retired to the back country and lived in a wigwam."

1782: The Life of Benjamin Franklin, Written by Himself

Benjamin Franklin lived from 1706 to 1790. Scientist, author, statesman, Declaration of Independence co-drafter, Ben Franklin also became a ceaseless traveler, mostly in the line of duty. His journals of the year 1782, published in London (1884), dealt with the important political events of the times, along with Franklin's travels. Here is a brief sampling:

Passy *9 May, 1782*

As since the change of the ministry in England some serious professions have been made of their dispositions to peace, and of their readiness to enter into a general treaty for that purpose; and as the concerns and claims of five nations are to be discussed in that treaty, which must therefore be interesting to the present age and to posterity, I am inclined to keep a journal of the proceedings as far as they come to my knowledge; and, to make it more complete, I will first endeavour to recollect what has already past. Great affairs sometimes take their rise from small circumstances. My good friend and neighbour Madame Brillon, being at Nice all last winter for her health, with her very amiable family, wrote to me, that she had met with some English gentry there, whose acquaintance proved agreeable. Among them she named Lord Cholmondely, who she said had promised to call on his return to England, and drink tea with us at Passy.

17 May, 1782

"1. That the British troops shall be withdrawn from the Thirteen Provinces of North America, and a truce made between Great Britain and the said Provinces, for years. (Suppose ten or twenty years.)

"2. That a negotiation for peace shall bona fide be opened between Great Britain and the allies of America.

"3. If the proposed negotiation between Great Britain and the allies of America should not succeed so far as to produce peace, but that war should continue between the said parties, that America should act, and be treated, as a neutral nation.

"4. That, whenever peace shall take place between Great Britain and the allies of America, the truce between Great Britain and America shall be converted into a perpetual peace, the independence of America shall be admitted and guaranteed by Great Britain, and a commercial treaty settled between them.

"5. That these propositions shall be made to the court of France, for communication to the American Commissioners, and for an answer to the court of Great Britain."

The same day Mr. Grenville visited me. He acquainted me that his courier was returned, and had brought him full powers in form to treat for a peace with *France and her allies.*

July 15

Set out about five in the morning; travelled till ten, then stopped to breakfast, and remained in the inn during the heat of the day. We had heard at the Cardinal's that our friend Mr. Holker, of Rouen, had been out that day as far as Port St. Antoine to meet us, expecting us there from a letter of M. de Chaumont's. Here came to us one of his servants, who was sent to inquire if any accident had happened to us on the road, and was ordered to proceed till he got intelligence. He went directly back, and we proceeded. We passed a chain of chalk mountains, very high, with strata of flints. The quantity that appears to have been washed away on one side of these mountains, leaving precipices of three hundred feet high, gives an idea of extreme antiquity. It seems as if done by the beating of the sea.

Tuesday, September 13

The wind springing fair last evening, after a calm, we found ourselves this morning at sunrising abreast of the lighthouse, and between Capes May and Henlopen. We sail into the bay very pleasantly; water smooth, air cool, day fair and fine.

We passed Newcastle about sunset, and went on near to Red Bank before the tide and wind failed, then came to an anchor.

Wednesday, September 14

With the flood in the morning came a light breeze, which brought us above Gloucester Point, in full view of dear Philadelphia! When we again cast anchor, to wait for the health officer, who, having made his visit and finding no sickness, gave us leave to land.

My son-in-law came with a boat for us; we landed at Market Street wharf, where we were received by a crowd of people with huzzas, and accompanied with acclamations quite to my door. Found my family well.

God be praised and thanked for all his mercies!

1811-1812: *Recollections of the Private Life of Napoleon by His Valet,* Constant

On occasion, the life of a famous person, in this case Emperor Napoleon Bonaparte, can be illuminated through the journals of someone close to him. Who were the people showing up at Napoleon's parties? Did Napoleon fall in love that year? And where did the Emperor find himself on a certain date? Constant, one of his personal valets, answers all these questions for us in a few short excerpts from a journal first published in 1895, and long since out of print.

September 11, 1811

His Majesty's attention was attracted by a charming young person one morning in the suburbs of Schoenbrunn; and some one was ordered to see this young lady, and arrange for a rendezvous at the château the following evening. Fortune favored his Majesty on this occasion. The éclat of so illustrious a name, and the renown of his victories, had produced a deep impression on the mind of the young girl, and had disposed her to listen favorably to the propositions made to her. She therefore eagerly consented to meet him at the château; and at the appointed hour the person of whom I have spoken came for her, and I received her on her arrival, and introduced her to his Majesty. She did not speak French, but she knew Italian well, and it was consequently easy for the Emperor to converse with her; and he soon learned with astonishment that this charming young lady belonged to a very honorable family of Vienna, and that in coming to him that evening she was inspired alone by a desire to express to him her sincere admiration. The Emperor respected the innocence of the young girl, and had her reconducted to her parents' residence, and gave orders that a marriage should be arranged for her, and that it should be rendered more advantageous by means of a considerable dowry.

October 14, 1811

This interview at Erfurt, which was so brilliant with illuminations, splendor, and luxury, ended on the 14th of October; and all the great personages whom it had attracted left between the 8th and the 14th of October.

This is the list of the principal persons.

The King of Bavaria.
The King of Würtemberg.
The King of Saxony.
The King and Queen of Westphalia.
The Prince Primate.
The Grand Duke and the Grand Duchess of Hesse-Darmstadt.
The Grand Duke and the Grand Duchess of Baden.
The Duke and the Duchess of Weimar.
The hereditary Prince of Weimar.
Prince Leopold of Saxe-Coburg.
The Duke of Saxe-Gotha.
The Duke of Oldenburg.
Prince William of Prussia.
The Prince of Mecklenburg-Schwerin.
The Prince of Mecklenburg-Strelitz.
The Prince of Anhalt-Dessau.
The Prince of Waldeck.
The Prince of Laleyen.
The Prince of Reuss.
The Prince of Ebersdorff.
The Prince of Gera.
The Prince of Schleitz.
The Princess de la Tour and Taxis.
The Prince of Salm-Dyck, *aide-de-camp* of the King of Würtemberg.
The Prince of Hohenlohe-Kirkberg, *idem.*
The Prince of Salm-Salm.
The Prince of Schaumburg.
The Prince of Bernburg.
The Prince of Isemburg.
The Prince of Rudolstadt.
The Prince of Hohenzollern-Sigmaringen.

Duke William of Bavaria.
The Duchess of Hildburghausen.
The Countess of Truxès.
The Count and Countess of Bochols.
The Count of Mongellaz.
The Count of Wurtemberg.
The Count of Reuss.
The Baron Vincent.
The Duke of Mondragone.
The Duke of Birkenfeld.
The Count of Goerliz, grand equerry of the King of Würtemberg.
The Count of Taube, prime minister, *idem*.
The Count de Dille, *aide de camp*, *idem*, etc.

November 3, 1811

Added to the fatigue of these repeated journeys, all conspired to produce feelings of intense sadness, which was reflected on almost all the countenances of the Imperial household; while the officers said among themselves that the combats in the North were trifling compared with those that awaited us in Spain.

We arrived on the 3d of November at the chateau of Marrac, and four days after were at Vittoria in the midst of the French army, where the Emperor found his brother and a few grandees of Spain who had not yet deserted his cause.

The arrival of his Majesty electrified the troops; and a part of the enthusiasm manifested, a very small part it is true, penetrated into the heart of the king, and somewhat renewed his courage.

1893: *Captain Cook's Journal*

The journal was often pressed into the service of explorers, scientists, adventurers. Self-educated Captain James Cook, an Englishman, happened to be all of those: He was among the first men to map the St. Lawrence River and estuary; he explored the Newfoundland shoreline and pushed across the Pacific from Cape Horn in search of New Zealand. His best-known exploit, however, was his voyage around the world, which took three full years.

A short excerpt from the journal follows; it was published in 1893 by a small London firm. Captain Cook's descriptions could often be dry, limiting themselves to nautical information and land data. But in this case, the captain's diary packs great excitement in the manner of a Robinson Crusoe adventure:

> *Land in New Guinea* *September 1770*
> But we had no sooner landed than we saw the print of Men's feet fresh upon the sand, and a little way further we found a small Shed or Hutt, about which lay green shells of Cocoa Nutts. By this we were well assured that the inhabitants were not far off; nay, we thought we heard their Voices in the woods, which were so close and thick that we did not think it safe to venture in, for fear of an Ambuscade, as we had only a Boat's crew with us, a part of which were left to look after the boat, which lay about a ¼ of a Mile from the Shore. We therefore took a walk upon the Sea beach, but had not gone above 200 Yards before we were attack'd by 3 or 4 Men, who came out of the woods a little before us, but upon our firing upon them they retir'd. Finding that we could not search the Country with any degree of Safety, we return'd to the boat and was followed by 60, or, as some thought, about 100, of the Natives, who had advanced in small parties out of the woods; but they suffer'd us to go to our boats without giving us any trouble. We had now time to view them attentively; we thought them to be about the size and Colour of the New Hollanders, with short, Cropt Hair, and quite naked like them. I thought these of a lighter Colour; but that may be owing to a whitish Pigment with which we thought their bodies were painted, because some appeared darker than others.

Their Arms were ordinary darts of about 4 feet long, made of a kind of reed, and pointed at one end with hard wood; but what appear'd more extraordinary to us was something they had which caused a flash of fire or smook, very much like the going off of a pistol or small Gun, but without any report. The deception was so great that people in the Ship actually thought that they had fire Arms; indeed, they seem'd to use these things in imitation of such, for the moment the first man we saw made his appearance he fir'd off one of these things, and while we lay looking at them in the boat 4 or 5 would let them off all at once, which had all the appearance in the world of Volleys of Small Arms; but I am confident that nothing came from them but smook, but by what means this was done, or what purpose it answer'd, we were not able to Guess. I thought the Combustable matter was contain'd in a reed or piece of small Bamboo, which they gave a Swing round in the hand and caused it to go off.

This place lies in the Lat. of 6° 15′ S., about 65 Leagues to the N.E. of Point St. Augustine, or Walsche Caep, and is near to what is called in the Charts by the long name of C. de la Colta de St. Bonaventura.

1912: *Captain Scott's Last Expedition*

Capt. Robert Falcon Scott's legacy remains with us forever. R. F. Scott was one of the first people to explore inhospitable Antarctica via a land route; his two expeditions introduced the use of dog sleds. And Scott gave the world details about many giant mountain ranges that had been seen only from the sea. Scott's feats included travel across the South Pole's great icecap. He actually reached the Pole on January 18, 1912, but died on his way back to civilization.

We would never have known about his ordeals

were it not for his diaries, which were found by search parties eight months later. Entitled *Scott's Last Expedition,* the journals were published in London by John Murray and are now out of print.

Some of R. F. Scott's last harrowing days emerge from the following excerpts:

> *Friday, March 16 or Saturday, 17, 1912*
>
> Lost track of dates, but think the last correct. Tragedy all along the line. At lunch, the day before yesterday, poor Titus Oates said he couldn't go on; he proposed we should leave him in his sleeping-bag. That we could not do, and induced him to come on, on the afternoon march. In spite of its awful nature for him he struggled on and we made a few miles. At night he was worse and we knew the end had come.
>
> Should this be found I want these facts recorded. Oates' last thoughts were of his Mother, but immediately before he took pride in thinking that his regiment would be pleased with the bold way in which he met his death. We can testify to his bravery. He has borne intense suffering for weeks without complaint, and to the very last was able and willing to discuss outside subjects. He did not—would not—give up hope to the very end. He was a brave soul. This was the end. He slept through the night before last, hoping not to wake; he woke in the morning—yesterday. It was blowing a blizzard. He said, "I am just going outside and may be some time." He went out into the blizzard and we have not seen him since.
>
> I take this opportunity of saying that we have stuck to our companions to the last. In case of Edgar Evans when absolutely out of food and he lay insensible, the safety of the remainder seemed to demand his abandonment, but Providence must fully removed him at this critical moment. He died a natural death, and we did not leave him till two hours after his death. We knew that poor Oates was walking to his death, but though we tried to dissuade him, we knew it was the

act of a brave man and an English gentleman. We all hope to meet the end with a similar spirit, and assuredly the end is not far.

I can only write at lunch and then only occasionally. The cold is intense, -40° at midday. My companions are unceasingly cheerful, but we are all on the verge of serious frostbite and though we constantly talk of fetching through I don't think anyone of us believes it in his heart.

Sunday, March 18

Today, lunch, we are 21 miles from the depot. Ill fortune presses, but better may come. We have had more wind and drift from ahead yesterday; had to stop marching; wind N.W., force 4, temp. -35°. No human being could face it, and we are worn out nearly.

My right foot has gone, nearly all the toes—two days ago I was proud possessor of best feet.

Thursday, March 22 and 23

Blizzard bad as ever—Wilson and Bowers unable to start—tomorrow last chance—no fuel and only one or two of food left—must be near the end. Have decided it shall be natural—we shall march for the depot with or without our effects and die in our tracks.

Thursday, March 29

Since the 21st we have had a continuous gale from W.S.W. and S.W. We had fuel to make two cups of tea apiece and bare food for two days . . . . Every day we have been ready to start for our depot 11 miles away, but outside the door of the tent it remains a scene of whirling drift. I do not think we can hope for any better things now. We shall stick it out to the end, but we are getting weaker, of course, and the end cannot be far.

It seems a pity, but I do not think I can write more.

R. Scott

For God's sake look after our people.

1942-1944: The Diary of Anne Frank

The tragedies of World War II were recorded in a great number of journals including those of the German pastors and priests imprisoned by the Hitler regime. As noted earlier in this book, one of the most remarkable diaries of the period was written by a Dutch teenager, Anne Frank, while hiding from the Nazis in Holland. She used school exercise books and addressed her frequent entries, in letter form, to a nonexistent friend named Kitty. Anne wrote with great simplicity and innocence, sharing much of what she saw and thought with "Kitty," maturing in the process.

The diary is that of a sensitive, affectionate, loving, and longing human being—one whom we still mourn today. For in August 1944, after two full years in the "Secret Annexe" of an Amsterdam house, Anne Frank and her Jewish family were arrested by the German police and shipped off to various concentration camps. Anne died at Bergen-Belsen in March 1945, just a few weeks before the war's end. Her diary was later found on the floor of the family's house; it seemed of no value to the plundering gestapo.

Later published by Otto H. Frank, her father, *The Diary of a Young Girl* has sold more than 15 million copies in 50 languages and remains one of the most important wartime documents. The excerpts are reprinted with the kind permission of Doubleday & Company and Otto H. Frank, who has held the copyright since 1952.

Saturday, 20 June, 1942

Hence, this diary. In order to enhance in my mind's eye the picture of the friend for whom I have waited so long, I don't want to set down a series of bald facts in a diary like most people do, but I want this diary itself to be my friend, and I shall call my friend Kitty. No one will grasp what I'm talking about if I begin my letters to Kitty just out of the blue, so albeit unwillingly, I will start by sketching in brief the story of my life.

Wednesday, 24 June, 1942

Dear Kitty,

It is boiling hot, we are all positively melting, and in this heat I have to walk everywhere. Now I can fully appreciate how nice a tram is; but that is a forbidden luxury for Jews—shank's mare is good enough for us. I had to visit the dentist in the Jan Luykenstraat in the lunch hour yesterday. It is a long way from our school in the Stadstimmertuinen; I nearly fell asleep in school that afternoon. Luckily, the dentist's assistant was very kind and gave me a drink—she's a good sort.

We are allowed on the ferry and that is about all. There is a little boat from the Josef Israelskade, the man there took us at once when we asked him. It is not the Dutch people's fault that we are having such a miserable time.

Wednesday, 8 July, 1942

Yes, I'm still alive, indeed, but don't ask where or how. You wouldn't understand a word, so I will begin by telling you what happened on Sunday afternoon.

At three o'clock (Harry had just gone, but was coming back later) someone rang the front doorbell. I was lying lazily reading a book on the veranda in the sunshine, so I didn't hear it. A bit later, Margot appeared at the kitchen door looking very excited. "The S.S. have sent a call-up notice for Daddy," she whispered. "Mummy has gone to see Mr. Van Daan already." (Van Daan is a friend who works with Daddy in the business.) It was a great shock to me, a call-up; every one knows what that means. I picture concentration camps and lonely cells—should we allow him to be doomed to this? "Of course he won't go," declared Margot, while we waited together. "Mummy has gone to the Van Daans to discuss whether we should move into our hiding place tomorrow. The Van Daans are going with us, so we shall be seven in all." Silence. We couldn't talk any more thinking about Daddy, who, little knowing what was going on was visiting some old people in the Joodser Invalide; waiting for Mummy, the heat and suspense, all made us very overawed and silent.

Suddenly the bell rang again. "That is Harry," I said. "Don't open the door." Margot held me back, but it was not necessary as we heard Mummy and Mr. Van Daan downstairs, talking to Harry, then they came in and closed the door behind them. Each time the bell went, Margot or I had to creep softly down to see if it was Daddy, not opening the door to anyone else.

Margot and I were sent out of the room. Van Daan wanted to talk to Mummy alone. When we were alone together in our bedroom, Margot told me that the call-up was not for Daddy, but for her. I was more frightened than ever and began to cry. Margot is sixteen; would they really take girls of that age away alone? But thank goodness she won't go, Mummy said so herself; that must be what Daddy meant when he talked about us going into hiding.

Thursday, 9 July, 1942

Dear Kitty,
So we walked in the pouring rain, Daddy, Mummy, and I, each with a school satchel and shopping bag filled to the brim with all kinds of things thrown together anyhow.

We got sympathetic looks from people on their way to work. You could see by their faces how sorry they were they couldn't offer us a lift; the gaudy yellow star spoke for itself.

Only when we were on the road did Mummy and Daddy begin to tell me bits and pieces about the plan.

For months as many of our goods and chattels and necessities of life as possible had been sent away and they were sufficiently ready for us to have gone into hiding of our own accord on July 16. The plan had had to be speeded up ten days because of the call-up, so our quarters would not be so well organized, but we had to make the best of it. The hiding place itself would be in the building where Daddy has his office.

Tuesday, 29 September, 1942

Dear Kitty,
Extraordinary things can happen to people who go into hiding. Just imagine, as there is no bath, we use a washtub and because there is hot water in the office (by which I always mean the whole of the lower floor) all seven of us take it in turns to make use of this great luxury.

But because we are all so different and some are more modest than others, each member of the family has found his own place for carrying out the performance. Peter uses the kitchen in spite of its glass door. When he is going to have a bath, he goes to each one of us in turn and tells us that we must not walk past the kitchen for half an hour. He seems to think this is sufficient. Mr. Van Daan goes right upstairs; to him it is worth the bother of carrying hot water all that way, so as to have the seclusion of his own room. Mrs. Van Daan simply doesn't bathe at all at present; she is waiting to see which is the best place. Daddy has his bath in the private office, Mummy behind a fire guard in the kitchen; Margot and I have chosen the front office for our scrub. The curtains there are drawn on Saturday afternoons, so we wash ourselves in semi-darkness.

Thursday, 1 October, 1942

Dear Kitty,
I got a terrible shock yesterday. Suddenly at eight o'clock the bell rang loudly. Of course, I thought that someone had come: you'll guess who I mean. But I

calmed down a bit when everyone said it must be some urchins or perhaps the postman.

The days are becoming very quiet here. Lewin, a small Jewish chemist and dispenser, works for Mr. Kraler in the kitchen. He knows the whole building well and therefore we are always afraid that he'll take it into his head to have a peep in the old laboratory. We are as quiet as mice. Who, three months ago, would ever have guessed that quicksilver Anne would have to sit still for hours—and, what's more, could?

Monday, 22 May, 1944

I hope *one* thing only, and that is that this hatred of the Jews will be a passing thing, that the Dutch will show what they are after all, and that they will never totter and lose their sense of right. For anti-Semitism is unjust!

And if this terrible threat should actually come true, then the pitiful little collection of Jews that remain will have to leave Holland. We, too, shall have to move on again with our bundles, and leave this beautiful country, which offered us such a warm welcome and which now turns its back on us.

I love Holland. I who, having no native country, had hoped that it might become my fatherland, and I still hope it will!

Yours, Anne

1974: *Pilgrim at Tinker Creek* by Annie Dillard

Most of us are able, once in awhile, to sit back and ponder the world around us. Most of us, too, can write down some of our observations and thoughts. But it takes an Emerson, a Merton, a Muir, a Thoreau—or an Annie Dillard!—to suffuse such words with uniqueness, with brilliance. Annie Dillard, essayist and diarist, has that writing talent that is all too rare. Here she demonstrates it in some brief selections from *Pilgrim at Tinker Creek,* by Annie Dillard 1974, reprinted by permission of Harper & Row.

> The birds have started singing in the valley. Their February squawks and naked chirps are fully fledged now, and long lyrics fly in the air. Birdsong catches in the mountains' rim and pools in the valley; it threads through forests, it slides down creeks. At the house a wonderful thing happens. The mockingbird that nests each year in the front-yard spruce strikes up his chant in high places, and one of those high places is my chimney. When he sings there, the hollow chimney acts as a soundbox, like the careful emptiness inside a cello or violin, and the notes of the song gather fullness and reverberate through the house. He sings a phrase and repeats it exactly; then he sings another and repeats that, then another. The mockingbird's invention is limitless; he strews newness about as casually as a god. He is tireless, too; toward June he will begin his daily marathon at two in the morning and scarcely pause for breath until eleven at night. I don't know when he sleeps.
>
> * * *
>
> . . . The road is vacant, the interstate is out of sight and earshot. I have hazarded into a new corner of the world, an unknown spot, a Brigadoon. Before me extends a low hill trembling in yellow brome, and behind the hill, filling the sky, rises an enormous mountain ridge, forested, alive and awesome with brilliant blown lights. I have never seen anything so tremulous and live. Overhead, great strips and chunks of cloud dash to the northwest in a gold rush. At my back the sun is setting—how can I not have noticed before that the sun is setting? My mind has been a blank slab of black asphalt for hours, but that doesn't stop the sun's wild wheel. I set my coffee beside me on the curb; I smell loam on the wind; I pat the puppy; I watch the mountain.

My hand works automatically over the puppy's fur, following the line of hair under his ears, down his neck, inside his forelegs, along his hot-skinned belly.

Shadows lope along the mountain's rumpled flanks; they elongate like root tips, like lobes of spilling water, faster and faster. A warm purple pigment pools in each ruck and tuck of the rock; it deepens and spreads, boring crevasses, canyons. As the purple vaults and slides, it tricks out the unleafed forest and rumpled rock in gilt, in shape-shifting patches of glow. These gold lights veer and retract, shatter and glide in a series of dazzling splashes shrinking, leaking, exploding. The ridge's bosses and hummocks sprout bulging from its side; the whole mountain looms miles closer; the light warms and reddens; the bare forest folds and pleats itself like living protoplasm before my eyes, like a running chart, a wildly scrawling oscillograph on the present moment. The air cools; the puppy's skin is hot. I am more alive than all the world.

* * *

I wonder how long it would take you to notice the regular recurrence of the seasons if you were the first man on earth. What would it be like to live in open-ended time broken only by days and nights? You could say, "It's cold again; it was cold before," but you couldn't make the key connection and say, "It was cold this time last year," because the notion of "year" is precisely the one you lack. Assuming that you hadn't yet noticed any orderly progression of heavenly bodies, how long would you have to live on earth before you could feel with any assurance that any one particular long period of cold would, in fact, end? "While the earth remaineth, seedtime and harvest, and cold and heat, and summer and winter, and day and night shall not cease": God makes this guarantee very early in Genesis to a people whose fears on this point had perhaps not been completely allayed.

1979: *Recovering: A Journal* by May Sarton

May Sarton, poet, novelist, nonfiction author, must also be considered one of the century's greatest diarists. More than any other writer, May Sarton infuses her diaries with a sense of humanity. She is both sensitive and wise and at once kind and deep. She understands nature, too.

The following excerpts are reprinted from her *Recovering: A Journal,* with permission of W. W. Norton, Co., 1980 by May Sarton.

> *Monday, February 26*
>
> I have been sitting for minutes watching the waves break over the end of the field. It is exciting when this happens because it means a big storm. This is a real Nor'easter, blowing a mixture of sleet, rain, and snow that is going to make for a precarious sortie to get the mail this morning. There is a total eclipse of the sun, which we won't see, of course, but that means a very high tide, two or three feet higher than normal at ten this morning. From my window here in my study I get a wide expanse of ocean, and, as I can't see the rocks below the field, it looks now as though the waves were running right over it, spreading their foam on the snow.

> *Saturday, May 3*
>
> My sixty-seventh birthday. A perfect, still day, sunshine for a change, and an unutterable blue, pale Fra Angelico sea. The daffodils are out in great garlands, lighting up the dark-brown field, and inside the fence there is a border of hyacinths, scillas, a few daffodils, and a trout plant just coming out, brilliant as the border in a tapestry. Against the wall on the terrace I did get the pansies in, and now the blue windflowers are coming out.

Monday, August 27

The problem is perhaps to learn how to come to a full stop. I am lucky enough to be able to do this by lying down for an hour in the afternoon, my way of making a shift from one kind of work to another. But someone with a full-time job can't take that way, and now and then I am too on edge, too dispersed by visits and the pile-up on my desk, to let go. That happened the other day, so I got up and went out into the garden to pull weeds for an hour and it was wonderful to feel the whole nervous system quieting down. When I am gardening I do not think of anything at all; I am wholly involved in the physical work and when I go in, I feel whole again, centered.

Tuesday, September 18

I have the feeling these days of returning from a long journey back to myself and my life here as it was two or three years ago, of coming *home* into my own ethos at last after a long interruption. So I wake full of excitement at the morning before me and all I hope to do within its brief hours. The golden autumnal days continue like a blessing, although it is now very dry and I see leaves wilting even on perennials. Yesterday afternoon I threw duties to the winds and went out to water the clematis along the fence, one of the glories of this place.

Wednesday, September 20

I have been thinking about the image of a journey as the image for a love affair and its ending as the coming home to one's self again. The value of loving someone passionately, often a person very unlike oneself, is that one is taken literally out of one's self on a journey into unknown territory. As in a journey to a foreign country there is culture shock; one often feels lonely, even attacked by the differences. One is also all the time in a state of strange excitement, there are glorious moments, unforgettable scenes that make one tremble with joy and surprise, and there are days of great fatigue when all one longs for is home, to be with the familiar that does not ask for stretching to understand it, which can be taken for granted. Where one can rest.

1980: *Diary of a Spiritual Mountain Summer,* by Frances Atkinson

One day, Colorado author Frances Atkinson decided to retreat to her mountain cabin for five weeks. She took her diary along. And here she set down, in simple words, what she felt and saw. The account of her mountain sojourn is so well written that her words brought an immediate echo to the heart and mind of her *Unity Magazine* editor. More, even one of the typesetters "literally glowed" as she put the material into print. The diary combines Thoreau-like nature observations with an inner search—and discovery!—of spiritual renewal.

The excerpts are reprinted with permission from *Unity: A Way of Life,* Unity Village, MO 64065, August 1980.

> Here I am, alone in a mountain cabin for five weeks, without even my dog to protect me or to keep me company. I have chosen to be here. My daughter and my two sons are grown now, and I have wanted for some time to enjoy the beauty of the mountains in an uninterrupted way. I feel a need to be free of the noise and hurry of the city. But most important, I *must* be away to "regroup" emotionally; within myself I am grieving because my recent marriage plans did not work out.
>
> In my hideaway I am living above the mountain towns—beyond even the end of the paved roads. Along the main gravel road near me are roomy meadows of tall grass for the horses of nearby ranch owners, and acres and acres of wild flowers, aspen,

and tall evergreens of all varieties. From my front window I look out upon an idyllic panorama: baby aspen in my front yard; hedges and clumps of wild roses; gorgeous columbine growing among other wild flowers of every size, shape, and hue. And not far distant, a mountain with the bluest of skies above. All this is framed by the tall pines and graceful blue spruce close to my cabin.

The beauty is beyond my wildest dreams. How incredibly fortunate I am!

The high paths of jet airliners do not come near here. I have brought no TV, and my one source of music in the cabin, my portable FM radio-cassette player, has a problem. Only a few minutes ago the water came on again, after not working for several hours.

Suddenly I realize I am really on my own. I, who have spent much time in the practice of meditation, am beginning to wonder: Can I stick this out for five weeks?

Slowly I sit down in a comfortable chair and let my body go limp. I breathe deeply. And I relax into the silence—physically, mentally, emotionally. Now I gather the stillness around me like a soft, luxurious cloak. I shall reach within myself for peace . . . for music . . . for healing . . . for appreciation of life, and for joy.

* * *

I am flexing my emotional muscles by shifting their way focus afrom my problems and onto, instead, the beauty around me! It is an exciting experience, for it gives me a marvelous tool from now on for overcoming the tense effects of mixed-up feelings. I can use this tool *on purpose* now, as well as accidentally—and that too is exciting! Dispelling an emotional trauma by focusing on something lovely? It works. I intend to keep using these new muscles.

And then my second awareness: in Nature's own quiet way, the wild flowers are showing me that they are not afraid to just stand up and *be*—even when they've been stepped on. They may appear fragile and vulnerable, but on those tiny, filamentlike stems they stand "tall" in their own knowingness. Each moment they are being fully themselves, and in so doing they provide nectar for the bees as well as beauty and fragrance for us. They are fulfilling their reason for being. This gives me fresh inner strength. For I too can stand tall and know my own worth even when I feel I've been trampled. I can have the silent courage to be me, as the flowers do. Isn't this emotional muscle-tuning?

Now the splendor of the morning took form. The rising sun had reached its horizon of mountaintops, and over these eastern peaks hung a bank of gleaming, silvery clouds.

Suddenly a cosmic prism appeared, with silver strands of light reaching giant fingers to the meadow below the mountaintops. We were awed, for we stood beside that very meadow receiving into ourselves this gift of shimmering beauty. It was as though the clouds were parting to reveal ladders of light, connecting heaven and Earth. Angels could have appeared on those streams of glory and I wouldn't have been surprised!

Some familiar words are coming to me now. I have read and heard them many times, but I feel because of this morning's experience that they are a new and fresh part of my own personal life:

"The heavens declare the glory of God,
And the earth shows forth his handiwork!"

* * *

One of the most amazing times to walk in a mountain forest is after a rain. Nature seems to be most silent then; it is as though the Earth and the wild flowers and the trees are quietly but busily absorbing.

Last evening I walked, unknowing, toward my miracle. The gravel road not far from my cabin winds beside a large, lush meadow. As I walked, deep purple blossoms, resembling the larger domesticated phlox, nodded at me from a roadside ravine; and I noticed that these wild beauties grew on stems three and four feet tall—the tallest wild flowers I'd seen. Standing there beside them to drink in their velvety perfection, I slowly became aware, in the lively silence, of the sound of water. It was a soft, flowing sound. Not visible, the stream I was hearing obviously came from the bottom of the roadside ravine. From this life-giving source, it was as though the gorgeous wild blossoms had pushed up to their unusual height in order to bless the countryside!

And so I walked on toward my miracle—again unknowingly. Coming to the end of the road I turned back, retracing my steps to return to my cabin. Intermittently that day I had been dealing with finances at my desk. In spite of my present preoccupation with the beauty around me, some worry. . . .

* * *

Epilogue

I look back over my five weeks. It surprises me now that I actually wondered at first if I could "stick it out." For at this moment, I am finding it almost unbearable to think of leaving "my" cabin, my plant and animal and insect friends, my mountains, and the incredible night sky, which takes on an entirely new character and depth when one is away from city lights.

My mountain summer, with its aloneness both a poignant sorrow and an uplifting joy, brought me discoveries galore! I shall never be quite the same of course after petting a butterfly—nor after reveling in both the glory of a mountain dawn and the potent silence of a freshly washed forest. The sudden appearance of that great clump of gorgeous out-of-season columbine will forever be to me a symbol of the limitless abundance of Nature. It spoke not only of abundant supply, but also of the kindly gift to us of abundant beauty. I reflect upon the fact that God could have made this Earth a place of utilitarian bounty only, and that in itself would be cause enough for praising him. But to think that he presents to us daily gifts of beauty besides—oh, how blessed we are!

I have learned this summer to be more still and to listen more openly than ever before, for Nature teaches some of her most usable lessons in the silence. Perhaps the greatest lesson of all has been simplicity:

> A tree, if it is to raise its branches high, must have its roots sunk deep. So with us.
>
> To live is to bend and adapt—and then to resume one's upward growth.
>
> All creatures need a territory to call "home."
>
> All living things need companionship, and touching and stroking, and love.
>
> And all creatures need to give love, for giving is the continuing example of God in action.
>
> Each of us—flower, tree, insect, animal, human, star, planet—is an integral part of the balance and oneness of Nature.

These then, I write in my diary, are the simplest of life's basic truths. And I ask, are they not also the most profound?

8

The Diary and the Teacher or Parent

Why Diaries Are Being Used as Teaching Tools

Alert teachers have long used journal-writing at all educational levels, from elementary school to junior and senior high schools and college. Samuel Dreksler, who makes the most of journal-writing in his twelfth-grade English classes at the Pomona High School in Arvada, Colorado, first got the idea while still a university student. "Education departments pushed journal-keeping as a teaching method," Dreksler recalls. "Our professors felt that a journal would stimulate a free flow of ideas, and that such writing would crank up the student's creativity."

This is still true for high school English teachers.

Diary work stretches young minds. Such writing is active and not passive. And, of course, the journal always improves language skills.

Dreksler has employed this method for some six years in his eleventh- and twelfth-grade classes. He sees it as a form of composition writing; more, he later encourages his young people to use the journal entries as the basis for short story creation.

Dreksler feels that keeping a daily journal promotes thinking and that it forces the students to express themselves. For this reason, he chooses a daily theme. A different topic appears on the chalkboard each day.

For instance: "If you could be anything, what would you be?" or "If you could see the future, what would you see?" or "Describe snow to a blind person." The student can then develop these themes to his or her liking.

Dreksler's colleagues around the country agree that the diary can be helpful in many ways. John Malo, a former eleventh-grade teacher (and later principal) at Foreman High, in Chicago, Illinois, feels that a diary provides the teacher with an understanding of the student as well, which ultimately means better rapport. "We learn about the young person's inner conflicts and problems," says Malo. "The diary can give us a clue as to what goes on inside the teenager. And we learn about his and her beliefs and values, too."

Malo's favorite themes included an invitation to "Write About Your Friends." The teenager's exploration of personal relationships in writing can also prove invaluable to the parent and, of course, to the young individual who gains insight into the self.

This is one of the major points made by Dr. Trudy Helmlinger, a well-known psychotherapist and child counselor, and author of *After You've Said Goodbye,* a book that deals with human relationships. She tells teachers and parents:

> Diaries are therapeutic, psychologically, for their cathartic value as well as a vehicle for developing personal insight. When you write life events, thoughts, and feelings down on paper it helps you clarify your own thinking. It also gives you insight about your reactions and personality traits by logging events so that you can then recognize patterns more objectively. It's easier to see the tree when you're not in the middle of the forest.

Ira Progoff, the therapist and journal specialist, has often lectured to large groups of adolescents. He describes the diary as "an instrument like a hammer or scalpel—a tool to help you deal with times of change." Progoff also feels that "working in the journal can be a fulfilling experience in its own right, an art form, if you like. It's something you can do just for the pure pleasure of it. You can play with it. Improvise."

High School Classroom Application

Educators and mental-health experts agree that to be truly effective, the diary must become a daily classroom *habit*. Ten minutes of writing per day may be enough. The repetition helps promote the discipline of daily entries. In some schools, the teacher herself (or himself) sets the example and utilizes the ten minutes for her/his personal diary, which she or he shares with the class. Other teachers simply see the diary period as an ideal way to gain a few extra minutes for administrative work. John Chesky, a Georgetown (Kentucky) teacher explains: "Since incorporating the student's daily, in-class journal into my curriculum, I have discovered that the journal is not only a positive writing exercise for the student, but it is also a godsend for me, the teacher. In a class chock-full of individual needs that demand personalized attention, and in a school system complete with administrative details, I have found those ten minutes of journal-writing one way of finding the precious time I need to fulfill my professional responsibilities."

Some educators (and parents) encourage the reading aloud of journal sections; such readings should be voluntary, however. Never force a child onto the classroom stage. There will be enough students—the extroverts, the future actors/actresses, the "hams," the uninhibited ones—who welcome the opportunity to exercise their vocal chords. As a result, these young people become more articulate as writers and speakers.

How about the teacher privately reading the daily journal material? According to a survey of coast-to-coast educators, it all depends on the young person's wishes. Says one English teacher: "If a youngster doesn't want me to read a certain page, I respect such wishes. I have no right to intrude into a child's personal secrets. (A few students actually cover their pages against this intrusion.) On the other hand, a good relationship between teacher and students usually causes the removal of such obstacles. Most high schoolers show no resistance to having their classroom journals read. Samuel Dreksler of the Pomona High School, for instance, collects his students journals twice during each term and examines them. He states that he never had any "privacy" problems.

Should journals be graded? Most educators say that such grading ought to be of a positive and encouraging nature, especially if the student worked hard. Dreksler assigns a checkmark and a + (plus) for "very good work"; a checkmark for "adequate work"; and a checkmark and a - (minus) for a below-par writing effort. In the case of elementary school children, the experts recommend only the briefest of markings, such as an "O.K." for minimum effort and an "excellent" for children who do more than is expected of them.

The teaching profession holds differing opinions when it comes to marking up the journals with corrections. The same applies to parents, of course.

Should you improve the young writer's spelling? Substitute a better word? Insert punctuation? "Some teachers think you should," says Dreksler. "But I think this is controversial."

The warning makes sense, particularly in the case of an already reluctant diarist; too many corrective intrusions may slow down the creative effort. Other children may get discouraged by red ink or become self-conscious about their journal output. At this juncture, it would also be unwise to promote revision; the revising and self-editing of material will take place in college, or in adult writing groups. In the same sense, the young person should not yet be asked to condense or delete; this can come later.

On the other hand, the more secure, mature, articulate—in short, the *talented* youngster—will accept some guidance in spelling, grammar, and punctuation. Being motivated, such a teenager knows that writing becomes essential for future jobs, that the diary can serve as an excellent proving ground for future application letters, résumés, or in corporate communications. The talented young person will welcome the chance to practice, to improve his/her vocabulary.

In fact, such students often continue their journal-writing during family outings or vacation trips. By writing frequently, these diarists improve their grammar. They become more observant and express themselves more clearly.

One typical example comes from a teenage boy. Taken to southern Italy during a summer vacation by his parents, he later regaled the class with journal entries such as this one:

> Lodged in a labyrinthian hotel. Squirmed through the market mob and delighted in foreign items, strange mixes of produce and fish. Was persuaded by a rubicund fishmonger to try a dab of tiny, translucent catch, which was raw. Delicious and undoubtedly very nutritious. Lots of lemon-boiled artichokes. Dishes of octopus segments. A brute of a merchant wielded an evil cleaver, and with swift force he severed a big tuna. It was definitely one of the best market scenes I've ever witnessed.

This teenager had a bold way with words, trying out new ones, and offering no objections when the teacher later corrected his spelling.

The young writer easily found subjects for his diary mill. During the same vacation, while briefly on the island of Mykonos, his father suggested that he write about an adult he'd met. The result:

> I met an Englishman with round, bluish hands, and long legs. He claims to have trod 166 countries thus far in his travels. He lives in his own home alone watching the ocean, living frugally. On journeys afar he wears patched pants and five pairs of socks to keep his poor-circulated feet warm. His light-brown hair has given way partially to a sun-tanned scalp, making

> his forehead seem overly large above his tiny raisin eyes. He is a fanatic, perhaps, devout or ardent stroller, strutter. He has kept careful daily record of his mileage since he was 14 years old. He has walked in the neighborhood of 240,000 miles since he began keeping track! He ventured to compare the distance from the earth to the moon, 250,000, to his own feat.

History teachers have considered it beneficial to encourage students to delve into the diaries of important public figures. The understanding of American history, for instance, can be bolstered by the reading of George Washington's journals. In the same sense, advanced English classes regularly dissect the diaries of Virginia Woolf, Anaïs Nin, or the work of more current diarists such as Graham Greene. Likewise, high school science students can enter the results of certain experiments in their journals; one New Hampshire science class, for instance, made good use of individual journals to record various tests that had to do with the hazards of cigarette smoking. Specifically, the science instructor attached a fresh cow lung to a smoking machine. The class's blow-by-blow account of the blackening lung, and the accumulation of nicotine and noxious gases, later impressed students in other classes as well. Some of the journal material proved powerful enough to sway many teenagers in favor of nonsmoking, or caused them to quit the cigarette habit if it were already established.

The Diary: Elementary School Successes

Elementary school teachers—and parents—seem in almost total agreement about the usefulness of the daily journal. The youngest group often starts out with a mere calendar; the children get five minutes to mark up some important events, activities, or thoughts of the day. (The calendar is later shown to parents, too.)

By the third grade, the diary may take many forms. It can contain a series of poems, for instance, or consist of drawings.

One teacher cooks up an "All About Me" booklet for each child; other classes let the youngsters devise a title for their notebooks such as "Dear Diary" or "Dear Snoopy." (This works well for small children at home.)

At this stage, the daily journal entry need be no more than a sentence or two; the latter can be begun by the teacher ("Next Sunday, my family plans to—" or, "My favorite activity is—," and "Here's why—"). The younger children can also be stimulated to action by the teacher's suggesion of a good topic. Recurrent ones are:

- My neighborhood. What makes it different?
- My father's (mother's) job. What he (she) does all day.
- My best friend. What he/she is like and why we like each other.
- My school. How I see it—
- My favorite TV program and why.
- My best-loved Christmas (or Easter or birthday).
- My chores at home.
- What we eat at home and how it is cooked.
- A book I enjoyed reading.
- The weather.

Some young children need help in coming up with the right words. A Hadley, Massachusetts, elementary teacher, for instance, recalled the case of a youngster who "copied words from maps, brochures, newspaper articles, stories in his reading book, anything that happened to be at hand at journal time. He was almost a nonwriter. I let him copy. I felt it helped him to gain confidence, to work at word recognition, and to get handwriting practice. He eventually weaned himself away from these props, and now daily writes from thoughts in his mind."

Experienced teachers—and parents—will be tolerant when it comes to penmanship, writing only in capital letters, or spelling. Mary Lou Cutter, at a Massachusetts elementary school, makes it a point to approach the children with a positive attitude. She says: "As the children write, I often circulate around the room reading over their shoulders, and at first I made simple comments, such as 'Fun!,' 'Good idea!,' 'Mmmmm!,' or 'I've been there, too.' As time went on and they became more comfortable with daily writing, I comment on the positive aspects, also. 'C., your spelling is improving.' 'Oh, you're working on such an interesting story, W. When you are done, may we hear it?' 'Beautiful handwriting, G.' 'L., you remembered to capitalize *I* every time today. Good!'"

Apart from the teacher's occasional comments, there should be silence in the classroom, however.

The *teaching* aspects are generally kept separate from journal-writing, for which the youngsters use special spiral-bound books. A Wisconsin fifth- and sixth-grade teacher, though, admits that the journal can give some excellent clues as to whether "skills previously taught are being used." Her report ruefully concludes that "some spelling lessons are still in order, and the class will have to work on punctuation, contractions, and capitalization." A few journal examples:

> "Tonite we have religion and I dint practis my gitaur yet."
>
> "Last nite my unkel came I think snoopy dose not like him because he bit him in the legs."
>
> "It was a gud day everting went ok that all gudby."

For older elementary school children, improvement can come from the reading of famous diaries. The sixth grade of this particular Wisconsin school, for instance, read the *Diary of a Young Girl.* It proved to be an inspiration. Other schools have supported the children's interest in television by letting them create TV-style dialogue in their diaries. (As always, the entries must be dated, however.) Through practice, the diary thus helps Johnny (or Jane) not only to write but also to read; many younger children are eager to read their creations aloud. The applause of their peers surely adds to a child's self-worth and "image"; the diary presentation also makes the young reader stand out as an individual who thus becomes a more "real" person.

The diary process generally arouses children's interest and often leads to curiosity about grammar and spelling. And to be sure, diary-writing helps parents keep track of their youngsters and learn what goes on in school. A teacher at an Ohio elementary school puts it this way: "The diary has strengthened my communication with parents and helped them become much more aware of and involved in our programs. This kind of interaction naturally makes the kids feel that what they do at school is important."

The Teacher as Diarist

Interestingly, some educators have employed

diaries themselves to check up on their own classroom attitudes and teaching techniques. One of the earliest examples? In 1939, Julia Weber Gordon, a young New Jerseyite, began to keep a journal. It dealt with her daily experiences in a one-teacher school with thirty children, ages five to fifteen. How do you handle so many different levels under one roof at the same time? Her diary gives one fascinating illustration:

> We washed and carded wool, spun wool thread, wove the thread into dyes. A deep appreciation of our colonial ancestors developed. The children began to read labels in clothes; learned the various animal sources of wool; made a world map to show these; discovered the cost of these various wools and the reasons; got deeply into the Industrial Revolution, child-labor laws, the cotton industry, the problems of the South, Cotton Exchanges, the threat of the new synthetic fibers.

Julia Weber Gordon also monitored her teaching methods and experiments; these included involving the various age groups in the creation of their own newspaper, followed by a guided tour through the local paper. Another time, according to her diary, she invited the garden specialist from the state Agricultural Extension Service, who taught the children how to grow and store vegetables. Her notes were eventually published as *My Country School Diary*. It is still a compelling document today.

Another diary venture, this one by John Malo, the Illinois high school principal, focused briefly and eloquently on what Malo knows so well—the atmosphere at school. In his book, *Tranquil Trails,* he writes:

> *Tuesday after Labor Day.*
>
> It is Teacher Orientation Day. The faculty drifts into the beehive, whose chambers this day are unusually quiet.
>
> Today I can see in the bright eyes, tanned faces, and jaunty steps of fellow workers who chose the direction of peace by withdrawal from closed chambers, reprieve from the traffic dragon and harsh sounds. The memory of solitude and calm will sustain their enthusiasm and toleration-level for the foibles of their students in the days ahead.

But Malo, a naturalist, has other interests, too: he spends his free hours outdoors in the little-known woodlands, marshes, and wilderness enclaves of Chicago. There, along the banks of the Des Plaines River, he faithfully registers the ever-exciting plant and animal life. Tranquil Trails!

Malo is a teacher who shows his students—and the rest of us mortals!—what diary-writing can be all about.

Bibliography

Diaries and Journals

Bede, Carl, ed. *Selected Journals of Henry David Thoreau.* Baltimore: Johns Hopkins University Press, 1967.

Boswell, James. *The Private Papers of James Boswell.* London and New York: Oxford University Press, 1957.

Byrd, Richard E. *Alone.* New York: G. P. Putnam's Sons, 1938.

Captain Cook's Journal. London: E. Stock, 1893.

Captain Scott's Last Expedition. London: J. Murray, 1913.

Constant, *Recollections of the Private Life of Napoleon by His Valet.* London: Saalfield, 1895.

Diaries of George Washington 1748-1799. Millwood, New York: Kraus Reprint, 1925.

Dillard, Annie. *Pilgrim at Tinker Creek.* New York: Harper and Row, 1974.

Doig, Ivan. *Winter Brothers: A Season at the Edge of America.* New York: Harcourt Brace Jovanovich, 1980.

Ferrell, Robert H., ed. *The Eisenhower Diaries.* New York: W. W. Norton & Co., 1981.

Frank, Anne. *The Diary of a Young Girl.* New York: Doubleday, 1967. © 1952 by Otto H. Frank.

Gauguin, Paul. *Writings of a Savage.* New York: Viking, 1978.

Gide, André. *Journals.* New York: Vintage, 1947.

Gilman, William, ed. *Selected Writings of Ralph Waldo Emerson.* New York: Signet New American Library.

Hanser, Richard. *A Noble Treason: The Revolt of the Munich Students Against Hitler.* New York: G. P. Putnam's Sons, 1979.

Kollwitz, Käthe. *The Diaries and Letters of Käthe Kollwitz.* Chicago: Henry Regnery, 1955.

The Life of Ben Franklin Written By Himself. Philadelphia: J. B. Lippincott, 1884.

McPhee, John. *Coming into the Country.* New York: Bantam, 1979.

Malo, John. *Tranquil Trails.* Matteson, Ill.: Greatlakes Living Press, 1977.

Mansfield, Katherine. *The Journal of Katherine Mansfield.* New York: Fertia, 1975.

Nin, Anaïs. *The Diary of Anaïs Nin, Vol. I-VII.* New York: Harcourt Brace Jovanovich, 1971.

Powell, John Wesley. *Exploration of the Colorado River.* Edited by Mary C. Rabbitt, U.S.G.S., Washington, D.C.: U.S. Government Printing Office, 1978.

Progoff, Ira. *At a Journal Workshop.* New York: Dialogue House, 1975.

Rubin, Michael. *Men Without Masks: Writings from the Journals of Modern Men.* Reading, Massachusetts: Addison-Wesley, 1980.

Saint Augustine. *Confessions,* trans. by. R. S. Pine-Coffin, London: Penguin Classics, 1961.

Sarton, May. *Recovering: A Journal.* New York: W. W. Norton & Co., 1980.

Sarton, May. *Journal of a Solitude.* New York: W. W. Norton & Co., 1977.

Washington, George. *Day by Day.* Edited by Elisabeth Bryant Johnson, Boston: Houghton Mifflin & Co., 1925.

Woolf, Virginia. *A Writer's Diary.* New York: Harcourt Brace Jovanovich, 1973.

Reference Books

Roget, Peter. *Roget's International Thesaurus.* New York: Crowell, 1977.

Strunk, William, Jr. and White, E. B. *The Elements of Style.* New York: Macmillan, 1978, 1979.

Writing

Baldwin, Christina. *One to One: Self Understanding Through Journal Writing.* New York: M. Evans & Co., 1977.

Casewit, Curtis. *Freelance Writing: Advice from the Pros.* New York: Macmillan, 1974, 1980.

Casewit, Curtis. *Graphology Handbook.* Rockport, Massachusetts: Para-Research, 1980.

Mack, Karin and Skjei, Eric. *Overcoming Writing Blocks.* Los Angeles: Tarcher, 1979.

Self-knowledge

Bach, George R., and Deutsch, Ronald M. *Pairing.* New York: Avon, 1975.

May, Rollo. *Love and Will.* New York: W. W. Norton & Co., 1969.

May, Rollo. *Man's Search for Himself.* New York: W. W. Norton & Co., 1953.

Simon, Sidney B. *Meeting Yourself Halfway.* Niles, Illinois: Argus Communications, 1974.

About the Author

CURTIS W. CASEWIT has been associated for more than fifteen years with the Creative Writing Department of Colorado University, Denver Center. He has written for *Reader's Digest, Catholic Digest, Christian Single* and many other magazines; he has contributed to some fifty newspapers including *The New York Times,* Toronto *Star, Los Angeles Times,* San Diego *Union, Denver Post, Globe & Mail.* He has also authored some twenty books; his best-known works are *Freelance Writing: Advice from the Pros; The Mountain World; Keep It Legal: How to Avoid the Pitfalls of Copyright; Strategies for Getting the Job You Want Now* and *The Graphology Handbook.*